FIDUCIARY WISDOM

MANAGING RETIREMENT PLANS

to Meet Today's Challenges

T0107149

FIDUCIARY WISDOM

MANAGING
RETIREMENT
PLANS

to Meet Today's Challenges

YOUR GUIDE TO BUILDING A GREAT 401(k) OR
403(b) THAT LOWERS LEGAL RISK AND RAISES
EMPLOYEE ENGAGEMENT

G. DAVID BIDDLE, AIF®

Published by Advantage, Charleston, South Carolina.
Member of Advantage Media Group.

ADVANTAGE is a registered trademark, and the Advantage colophon is a trademark of Advantage Media Group, Inc.

Printed in the United States of America.

ISBN: 978-1-59932-653-5
LCCN: 2016952532

This publication is designed to provide accurate and authoritative information in regard to the subject matter covered. It is sold with the understanding that the publisher is not engaged in rendering legal, accounting, or other professional services. If legal advice or other expert assistance is required, the services of a competent professional person should be sought.

 Advantage Media Group is proud to be a part of the Tree Neutral® program. Tree Neutral offsets the number of trees consumed in the production and printing of this book by taking proactive steps such as planting trees in direct proportion to the number of trees used to print books. To learn more about Tree Neutral, please visit **www.treeneutral.com.**

Advantage Media Group is a publisher of business, self-improvement, and professional development books. We help entrepreneurs, business leaders, and professionals share their Stories, Passion, and Knowledge to help others Learn & Grow. Do you have a manuscript or book idea that you would like us to consider for publishing? Please visit **advantagefamily.com** or call **1.866.775.1696.**

Thank you, Valerie, for all the support.

TABLE OF CONTENTS

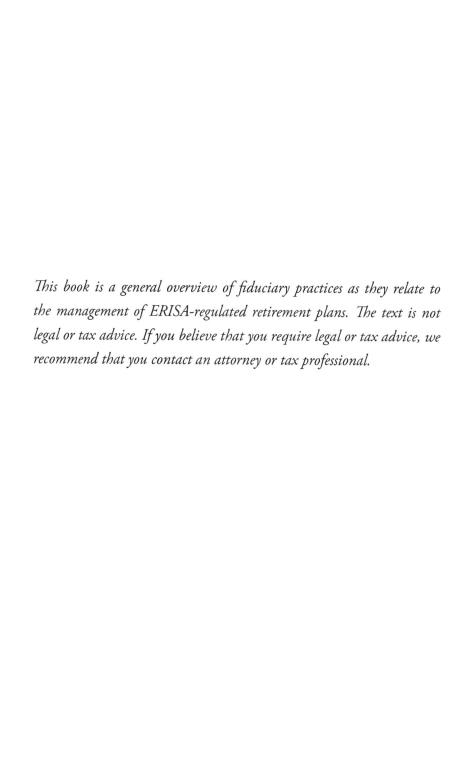

This book is a general overview of fiduciary practices as they relate to the management of ERISA-regulated retirement plans. The text is not legal or tax advice. If you believe that you require legal or tax advice, we recommend that you contact an attorney or tax professional.

FOREWORD
BY FRED REISH, ESQ.,
NATIONALLY KNOWN ERISA ATTORNEY

It is hard to properly manage a retirement plan. The Internal Revenue Code imposes complex qualification requirements. The Employee Retirement Income Security Act (ERISA) requires that employers act "prudently" in administering the plan, hiring service providers, determining and evaluating expenses, and selecting and monitoring investments. In performing those tasks, the responsible officers and managers are held to a high standard, sometimes called the "prudent expert rule." In fact, several courts have said "a full heart and an empty head" is not enough to be prudent.

Fortunately, the law permits plan sponsors to "hire" the expertise. That means that the sponsor must engage competent and qualified service providers for the plan—for example, an adviser, a recordkeeper, and an administrator. That should be done carefully. Experience is important because of the complexity.

However, it is not enough to just hire the expertise. Plan sponsors must understand how their plans work and oversee the providers. That requires a basic understanding of the design, administration, and investment of plans. That's why G. David Biddle's book, Managing Retirement Plans to Meet Today's Challenges, is an important tool for compliance. It's well written, conversational, easy to read, and uses real-world examples. He makes it clear this is not the end of your journey to compliance; instead, it's a starting point for understanding how to comply with the laws that govern you and your plan and how to use best practices to improve the results for your employees.

The Risks and the Rewards

"You don't understand—I *need* my money *now!*" the man on the phone shouted at me. He was a construction worker who had the misfortune of working for a Philadelphia-area company that was going belly up, a fate that befell a multitude of firms in that industry in the last decade.

Not only was he losing his job, but he was on the verge of losing his house to foreclosure unless he immediately could get his hands on his retirement plan savings. The company had brought me in to take over management of that 401(k) plan—and though the company was heading into bankruptcy, it was still responsible for doing right by the several dozen workers who had invested in the plan.

I tried to break the news to the man gently. "I'm sorry, I feel for you," I said, "but I can't send you your money just now. You see, what's happening . . ."

Salty language ensued. I assured him that his savings would come to him eventually, but he wasn't exactly in the mood for my explanation. "Who took my money?" he sputtered. "You guys don't even have it there anymore, do you?"

"Your money is still in your account," I explained, "but what we have to do . . ." I paused, realizing I was talking to silence. He had hung up.

Within an hour, I checked my voicemail to find a message from a woman identifying herself as a representative of the federal Department of Labor (DOL) in Philadelphia. She explained that she had spoken with a gentleman who claimed that his employer was keeping him away from his hard-earned savings. He believed the money had vanished. "Call me right back," the message said. "We need to talk—now."

I had been urging the company's owner to take prompt action to deal with the 401(k). The owner had troubles aplenty, both business and personal, that were distracting him from that responsibility, but he finally agreed that it was time to shut down the plan—after all, there would be no more company to support it. And so we had begun the arduous task.

The first step was relatively simple: the signing of a corporate resolution to dissolve the plan. Once a company does that, however, the individual participants no longer can withdraw their money at will. Instead, a single day must be scheduled for the distributions to all participants. Those are the rules, designed to protect the investments and return them to all participants in an orderly manner. It's done that way in the best interest of all. Still, individuals can be hurt.

That is what I was trying to explain to the irate caller, and that is what I discussed with the woman at the DOL when I returned her call. She understood the situation immediately. A few weeks earlier, that construction worker could have withdrawn his money freely, but not now. The only question was which of us would be following up with him. She volunteered.

It was a particularly troubling case to resolve. Several months passed before we could distribute the money. We had difficulty even finding about twenty former employees who had long since left for parts unknown but had not rolled over their accounts. We had to track those people down.

In hindsight, what I found most astounding was how swiftly the DOL responded to the complaint. You hear so much about the sluggish nature of government bureaucracy—but those folks were on it like a chicken on a June bug, as one of my long-ago teachers was fond of saying. They wasted no time in addressing the potential that somebody was being done wrong in the world of employer-sponsored retirement plans.

It is quite understandable that such a scenario does not tend to sit well with most employees, particularly when they learn that they will not be able to touch their money for a while. They worry. They suspect. They talk to their friends and neighbors, one of whom just might be a lawyer who is aware of the flood of recent litigation nationwide involving retirement plans.

Plan sponsors that have done no wrong can still find themselves embroiled in litigation. It didn't happen to that construction company—but it does happen. Even if the case never gets to court, sponsors can spend hundreds of thousands of dollars just to establish that they have upheld their fiduciary duties. Unfortunately, many sponsors aren't sure exactly how to comply with that standard.

Faced with such risks, many sponsors wonder whether they should just give up on the retirement plans that they set up in high hopes of attracting and keeping talented employees with a superlative benefit. I hear those grumblings regularly: "These lawsuits and these regulations are a nightmare," they say. "Maybe we should just shut this thing down. Why are we even doing this?"

Let me venture to say that they are doing this out of a sense of responsibility to the hard-working men and women who regularly and faithfully tuck away their money, dreaming of good days to come. The presumption of both employer and employee should be that a retirement plan will continue indefinitely. The intent, after all, should be to encourage regular, disciplined saving over the course of a long career. It's like a bond of faith. When that bond is abridged, for whatever reason, the fallout can be difficult. And yet we see it happening. How has it come to this?

AN ERA OF REGULATION AND LITIGATION

We are in an era of ever-increasing regulations that govern the operation of retirement plans. The regulations establish standards that must be met but do not provide clear direction on what to do. The sponsors and administrators must be alert to their fiduciary responsibility to act in the best interest of the participants. They need to take action to stay in the good graces of the law, but many of them do not know how. They do not truly understand what they are dealing with.

Companies also tend to have deep pockets, or at least that is the impression of those who are watching intently for any lapse in those fiduciary duties. Those who are adept at making widgets for profit are not necessarily as savvy when it comes to financial and legal issues of governing a retirement plan. Frankly, sometimes those who operate the plans do not even know that they are fiduciaries. They may not know what could happen if they fail to meet the increasingly strict expectations.

Here is what could happen: they could get sued, and they do—and for a lot of money. Anyone involved in the dealings and management of a retirement plan faces the potential of being held personally liable for a fiduciary breach. In recent litigation, settlements have forced employers to part with large sums of money in order to make employees, and their attorneys, "whole."

These are not isolated and unusual cases. In fact, only the tobacco and asbestos litigation has been outpacing the legal activity in the retirement space. The regulatory and legal atmosphere can feel so intimidating that it is little wonder that so many employers have become far less enthusiastic about offering retirement plans.

Here are just a few of the settlement figures that have been reported, along with the claims that were made by plan participants during the litigation. In the settlements, the corporations did not admit to any wrongdoing.

- **Lockheed Martin Corp.: $62 million, 2015**

  - Retirement plan participants accused the company of losing nearly $300 million of their investments. The suit alleged that Lockheed imprudently managed a fund option by putting too much of it in short-term money market investments.

- **Novant Health Inc.: $32 million, 2015**

  - Employees claimed the company had allowed millions of dollars in excessive administrative fees, squandering some of their retirement funds, without even shopping among third-party vendors to see if the price was fair.

- **International Paper: $30 million, 2013**

- According to the lawsuit, the company and some of its executives had misled 401(k) participants and concealed fees and had maintained its own stock as an imprudent investment option.

- **Kraft Foods Global Inc.: $9.5 million, 2012**

  - The lawsuit alleged that Kraft had allowed excessive fees in its retirement plans, kept too much cash in company stock funds, and offered investment options that were imprudent.

- **Bechtel Corp.: $18.5 million, 2010**

  - The engineering giant and its plan administrator subjected employee investments to unreasonable fees and expenses and offered imprudent investment options.

- **Caterpillar Inc.: $16.5 million, 2010**

  - Retirement plan administrators breached their fiduciary duty, the claim said, with investment options that had excessive and unreasonable fees. The employees alleged that administrators had made investments for their own benefit and had not made certain disclosures to participants.

- **General Dynamics Corp.: $15 million, 2010**

  - Employees who brought the suit claimed that excessive fees had been charged in the defense contractor's retirement plan and that plan assets had been used as seed money to build a for-profit business.

Those obviously are large and sophisticated companies. One might presume that they all have experienced executives at the helm—people with good minds and access to competent professionals in the various aspects of their financial and legal dealings. And they all paid out a bundle to settle claims from employees, who alleged either that their plans had excessive fees or that a lack of fiduciary oversight had seriously harmed their financial situation and prospects.

The retirement plans that those employers operate are huge, much larger than a typical plan, but the settlements tend to set a precedent. As attorneys become encouraged by the success of the litigation and see how much they can boost their business from such cases, it is likely that more and more smaller plans also will be targeted.

The best way to fight back is through knowledge. Employers large and small need to manage their plans to defend against the potential that a claim of fiduciary breach will be filed against them. Even if it never happens, the growing regulations are bound to prove increasingly costly. Most plans will need expert assistance to manage their governance and liability.

REDUCING RISKS, ENHANCING REWARDS

If you are reading this, you most likely are a sponsor of a retirement plan or a plan administrator. I wrote this book for you so that you can take whatever steps might be necessary to come into compliance, and to stay that way, before it is too late.

Don't let it happen to you. If you understand the regulations, you can take action to avoid the hundreds of millions of dollars in claims, fines, and attorney fees that others have paid. True, most of the litigation and audits have been focusing on the big companies with the multibillion-dollar plans, not on the smaller ones—typically of $20 million to $250 million. It's not as if the helicopters will be dropping on your office in the middle of the night as DOL commandos shout, "This is the 401(k) police, hit the floor!" You don't need a flak jacket, but you do need some basic oversight and governance to monitor your plan. The enforcers and the plaintiffs keep circling.

By sharpening your focus on plan operations, you will be doing more than protecting your company and fending off lawsuits. You will be further developing a top-quality plan for your employees. A staff that receives robust and valuable benefits tends to feel a greater sense of dedication and loyalty. Through your vigilance and oversight, you will be serving your business interests, and you will be serving your people and their families.

For nearly a quarter century, I have been working as an investment fiduciary. I started well before fiduciary became the hot topic that it is today in financial circles. In that role, I must always put my clients' best interests ahead of my own. My fiduciary experience started with advising individuals at retirement, and in 2005 I expanded into managing retirement plans.

Many things have changed since that time. Even a decade ago, a typical plan sponsor would simply place a binder from a 401(k) or 403(b) on a shelf and just send in the deposits after completing payroll. That was called management. Not anymore.

Over the years, I have strived to create systems and prudent processes to significantly improve the quality of retirement plans and to remove the risks that employers could face. The result has been the development of consistently successful plans that comply with regulations and that employers can manage more efficiently for greater gains. We reduce those risks and enhance those rewards—both at the same time.

IT'S TIME FOR ACTION

Success in managing a retirement plan is all about action: what you do, how you make decisions, and whom you consult for help. A quality plan needs a quality team. The right people, working together, can deliver a plan that you will be proud to offer. It will keep costs down and promote a more secure retirement for your employees. Without action, however, nothing happens.

If you have not been paying much attention to your plan or you want to optimize your plan, I urge you to keep turning these pages. In the chapters ahead, you will find suggestions for specific actions that you should be taking regularly. If you are currently monitoring your plan, then keep reading to learn about some valuable tools to help you prioritize your actions. You will find insights throughout on getting the best from your plan and from your team. You can also find a wealth of information on our website, www.fiduciarywisdom.com.

We will be taking a look, for example, at how to build that team and who should serve on it—and who should not. We will be examining the importance of offering an appropriate investment menu and the danger that you could face if you fail to give that selection your diligent attention.

We will be looking not only at 401(k) management but also the new rules for nonprofit organizations and their 403(b) plans. Though they differ somewhat in operational steps and requirements, both types fundamentally should be functioning in nearly the same way.

We will discuss, as well, the features of your plan document and how to evaluate the quality of your plan and of your service providers. And we will be looking at ways to educate the workforce and to keep open the lines of communication, so critical to success.

Let's get started. To fully grasp the significance of these matters, you must understand the basic rules and how those rules came to be. The context of history gives us a better appreciation of what is happening today, and it provides a perspective that is critical to serious plan management. A cavalier attitude leads to trouble.

The core regulations date back to the Employee Retirement Income Security Act (ERISA) of 1974, and there have been many developments in the decades since. As you will see, however, the push to protect workers had its genesis in something that happened more than a decade *earlier*.

CHAPTER ONE

The Rise of ERISA

The Studebaker-Packard Corporation had a problem. Unable to compete with the Big Three, the underdog automaker finally closed its Indiana factory in 1963, eliminating about seven thousand jobs. Studebaker would soon join the dozens of other automakers that had vanished since World War II—names like Nash, Duesenberg, and DeSoto. The company had started as a blacksmith and wagon maker in 1852. It began producing electric cars in 1902—Thomas Edison bought the second one that it made—and it rolled out gas-powered cars a few years later. Studebaker had reached great heights, but now it was in its death throes.

As the South Bend assembly line ground to a halt, so did the company's pension plan for its hourly workers. Thousands of those workers would get only a lump sum amounting to a small portion of the benefits that they had earned during their working years. Thousands of the younger workers would be getting nothing. The failed automaker did not have anywhere near the resources needed to satisfy legitimate benefit claims. In a time when pay raises were out of the question due to the company's financial struggles, Studebaker instead had thrown union workers the bone of generous pension benefits down the road. It did not, however, fund that promise.

The predicament of the Studebaker employees quickly became a national symbol of the need to reform pension plans operated by companies across the country. The shutdown gave the United Auto Workers an opportunity to push for legislation to address pension default risk and to require insurance against termination of plans. Washington policymakers had already been studying the issues. A similar failure of the Packard division in 1958 had raised concerns, and in 1961, President John F. Kennedy established a special committee to investigate private pension shortcomings. Now, national attention was focusing on the problem. Without protection, workers clearly could lose the retirement benefits that they had earned through hard work over many years.

The Studebaker pension default became the catalyst for legislative change. Congress eventually would enact a remedy, although it was a decade in the making. In 1974, it approved ERISA. This came on the heels of the increasing public attention, as evidenced in special reports on the major television networks, including NBC's hour-long *Pensions: The Broken Promise.* As support for pension reform grew, Congress held a series of public hearings, culminating in the passage of the legislation.

It was on Labor Day of 1974 when President Gerald Ford signed the bill into law, establishing standards for private-sector pensions and health-benefit plans. Among its provisions, ERISA required pension vesting after ten years of service. It held company and plan officials to fiduciary standards, and it required that they actually fund the plans they offered. It also required plan sponsors to acquire pension insurance to further protect employees.

ERISA has been repeatedly amended in the years since. Much has changed in more than four decades, but ERISA is still the foundation of pension-benefits law.

Since that time, we have left the era of pensions and have entered the era of the 401(k) and 403(b) and other defined-contribution plans. By offering their workers these plans, employers effectively have transferred to them the responsibility of preparing for their own retirement. Employees at companies large and small are taking on the risk of saving and investing their money, whether they are financially literate or not. Meanwhile, the defined-benefit plan, or pension, has become nearly extinct in the private sector. ERISA's original mission, to reform those pensions, has been shifting to new challenges.

COMPLEX AND CONFUSING RULES

In 1963, at the time of the Studebaker debacle, there were few laws—either at the federal or state levels—that regulated pension plans. A number of states soon started to enact legislation in hopes of preventing such pension defaults. The result was a patchwork of inconsistent and ineffective laws. Although ERISA sought to replace that patchwork, many of those laws remained in place. Some plans that were not subject to ERISA were nonetheless subject to the state laws, and that remains the case to this day.

In essence, ERISA provided for three fundamentals:

1. To require disclosure of financial and other plan information to the participants and beneficiaries

2. To establish standards of conduct for plan fiduciaries

3. To provide appropriate remedies for participants, including access to the federal courts

Unfortunately, the rules that govern those directives are opaque and complex. The guidelines and "goals" that ERISA establishes for plan managers are vague. To figure out how to meet those standards of conduct, plan fiduciaries must interpret the regulations. They must determine how they apply to their company's unique circumstances, and that can be a difficult task.

Adding to the challenge are the constant changes to ERISA. These are not generally in the form of formal changes to the law, but rather they are the result of court cases and the decisions and actions of the regulators and the enforcers—namely, the DOL, the Department of the Treasury (primarily the Internal Revenue Service [IRS]), and the Pension Benefit Guaranty Corporation. ERISA often refers not only to the federal act itself but also to the entire body of laws and regulations that deal with employee-benefit plans, many of which are also entwined in the Internal Revenue Code.

These agencies continue to shape the specifics of fiduciaries' responsibilities. The primary agency that reviews defined-contribution plan operations is the DOL. It sets out guidance for fiduciaries to reflect its interpretations of the law, and it performs audits of plans to determine levels of compliance. The IRS also can audit plans, but its focus is more on tracking the deposits and payments and not so much on the fiduciary processes.

The DOL has the ability to levy fines if it believes that it has discovered a significant fiduciary breach. The fines tend to be levied upon plan sponsors who have shown significant deficiencies in management. They may be fined in cases where fiduciary actions, or inactions, have resulted in real damage to plan participants. My goal for clients is to keep them far away from any possibility that they will be in such a situation.

By keeping a close watch on the DOL guidance, advisors and attorneys can determine the direction that the department will be moving. They can see the topics that will be the focus for the coming year and get a feel for how the department will be expecting fiduciaries to act. It is critical to understand the guidance because it clarifies the specific actions that plan sponsors should be taking.

THE CHANGING FOCUS FOR ERISA

Because ERISA's original aim was to regulate the traditional pensions, most of the details in the law addressed those defined-benefit plans, which paid out a regular amount to retirees every month. After all, it was the outcry over pension defaults that led to the legislation in the first place. The defined-contribution plans—the 401(k)s and the 403(b)s and similar tax-deferred programs—had yet to be invented.

They made their debut several years later. An obscure provision was added in 1978 to the Internal Revenue Code—Section 401(k)—allowing a tax break on deferred income. A few years later, some companies were offering employees the new tax-advantaged way to save for retirement through payroll deduction. A trickle became a torrent. Since the 1980s, the defined-contribution plans have spread far and wide.

Today, the defined-contribution plans have become a new focus for ERISA regulations. The regulations, of course, still do cover the traditional pensions—that is, those of them that remain. They are becoming increasingly rare in the private sector because employers find it expensive to maintain an effective pool of capital to pay the benefits. As people live longer, pension plans require ever more capital to maintain those payments for the lifetime of the retirees and often for the lifetime of their spouses as well.

Defined-contribution plans now are the typical vehicle that people use to save for retirement. The employee contributes to a personal account through payroll deductions, selecting from among a menu of investment options, and often receives a matching amount from the company. The employee gets an immediate tax deduction for the amount of his or her contribution. The account grows free of taxes until the money is withdrawn years later during retirement, when the income tax bracket presumably will be lower. After age seventy and a half, withdrawals are mandatory.

The sponsors of 401(k) plans generally are for-profit companies, corporations, sole proprietorships, and the like. The sponsors for 403(b) plans are nonprofit organizations, including school systems and universities. Recent changes in the law now allow nonprofit organizations to offer 401(k) plans. Again, 401(k) and 403(b) plans should fundamentally operate in nearly the same way.

When employees are responsible for choosing their own investments, they need to bring some level of insight to those selections—but they often don't. The typical employee is not an investment expert. Studies have shown that many employees tend to make poor investment decisions, resulting in returns much too low to bring them success in retirement.

The fact that employees have more responsibility for their own investments is a primary reason that the DOL has pushed for increased regulation of direct-contribution plans. To invest wisely, employees need the education and tools for success. The challenge for direct-contribution plans is to equip participants with what they need to make good choices.

A NEW ROUND OF REGULATIONS

The first comprehensive statutory update in forty-three years came after the passage of the Pension Protection Act of 2006 (PPA 2006), which made important changes to the way retirement plans are managed. The following year, the IRS and the DOL issued final regulations based on the law.

Many plans found that they needed to do a lot of work to bring operations into compliance with the law. Specifically, 403(b) plans needed to change their fiduciary management to bring their plans into parity with 401(k) plans. In my experience, the real impact of PPA 2006 was to bring all defined-contribution plans into a single management structure, with a process-based approach.

Here are just a few of the updates that PPA 2006 put forth:

- It established rules for investment advice to participants.

- It required an ERISA 5500 tax return for all plans, including 403(b) plans.

- It provided for civil penalties for some violations.

- It expanded requirements for disclosures to participants.

- It created a default investment procedure when participants fail to make selections.

- It established statutory support for automatically enrolling participants in plans.

I believe that PPA 2006 actually has made plan management simpler. By creating a twelve-month schedule for review and analysis, you can combine both management and compliance in one set of actions. Those actions, after all, are what truly matter. Good plan advisors are valuable because of the process they institute to help the sponsor. A quality advisor should be able to succinctly articulate that value to the employer and to the plan participants. When you interview advisors, ask them to explain their actions based on ERISA or PPA 2006 compliance. If they cannot do so, move on.

Recently, the regulators have been making a strong push for participants to understand the fees that are charged within their plan and for the fiduciaries to pay close attention to the monitoring of the plan.

The fee focus results from an impression expressed by many participants that their retirement plan is "free" to them. That of course is not the case. They are paying fees to support the operations and compliance measures that provide participants with the plan's tax advantages. Those fees should be appropriate and reasonable. Retirement plans must comply with many regulations that an individual's investment account does not face. Therefore, retirement plans (depending on the size) can be more expensive than a simple index fund that you can purchase directly.

Fiduciary oversight and monitoring has been an emphasis since the original ERISA law was drafted, but the Labor Department has been sharpening its focus on those responsibilities. Plan sponsors therefore need to sharpen their diligence. I have often found that a sponsor has done very little since setting up the plan years earlier. The sponsor has no real governance process, and the records are void of any monitoring. You would not call that a prudent management style.

HOW SAFE IS YOUR PLAYGROUND?

In operating a retirement plan, you should keep two things top of mind: your obligation to manage it prudently and your duty to your employees. These are consistent themes in the ERISA guidelines. It still surprises me when I find plan sponsors who make decisions that violate these basic tenets. Sometimes they do it for convenience. Sometimes it is a simple mistake. But every time, the consequences could be significant for both the employer and employees.

In short, plan fiduciaries can be held personally liable. ERISA is a unique law in many ways, including the ability of employees to receive damages after a fiduciary breach. In many areas of law, employers can "shelter" both personal and company assets, using various tools and structures. The intent is to encourage business speculation and growth. Such sheltering does not work under ERISA. When you can be held personally liable, you are likely to take plan management very seriously. We will explore this in more detail in chapter 4.

Imagine that you are managing a playground. Your responsibility is to make sure that the equipment is in good repair and that the fence is secure. You should offer a selection of quality equipment, refusing to allow anything questionable. If you come across any hazards, you should repair or remove them without delay. You should regularly inspect all areas of the playground and certify them as safe to use. You should make sure that nobody unsavory is hanging around the premises and that all the adults are of upstanding character and qualified as caretakers. These are the prudent things to do.

True, it still is possible that someone could get hurt on your playground through his or her own actions, particularly when using some of the riskier equipment. That would be unfortunate, of course, but you would not be held responsible—as long as you complied with all the requirements and regulations for providing a safe play area.

Managing a retirement plan certainly is no child's play. You are dealing with the retirement and dreams of your employees and their families. But the principles are similar. Your job is to do your best, within reason, to make sure that no one gets hurt. All of your actions and decisions must be in the best interest of everyone who is granted admission.

Think about it: How safe is your playground? When did you last conduct a full inspection?

NON-ERISA PLANS

Although most private retirement plans are subject to ERISA, the 403(b) plans sponsored by governmental and public-education employers may be exempt from the federal regulations. The 403(b) plans sponsored by religious organizations are exempt as well, although they may choose to come under ERISA coverage.

Nonprofit organizations also may be exempted from ERISA if they meet certain specific requirements. Nonprofits long preferred a non-ERISA plan because they were subject to less regulation. They did not have to file the Form 5500 and undergo annual audits, for example, and some of the fiduciary standards were less strict. To qualify, the sponsor could have only very limited involvement in operating the plan.

In recent years, however, as the IRS has sought to align 403(b) regulations with those used for 401(k) plans, compliance has become more challenging. The distinction between a non-ERISA and an ERISA 403(b) is becoming more blurred, and nonprofits run the risk of unintentional violations and penalties for breaching the requirements.

A surprising number of non-ERISA plans exist, including those sponsored by many churches and organizations with church affiliations. In my experience, many of the organizations that believe that they have a non-ERISA plan are actually covered by the federal regulations.

For example, let's say a true church is operating under a non-ERISA plan, often called a "steeple plan." It's retirement plan—for the pastor and a secretary and a couple of employees who do church work—is exempt from the regulations. Then the church opens a school that is closely tied to it—the pastor is the principal, and the school is part of the church's mission. Over time, however, the church realizes that the school will be easier to manage if it had its own board, and the school operations become independent from the church. The church no longer controls what is happening within the school operation. At that point, the pension plan would fall under ERISA, particularly if it is adding employer contributions.

In general, no pension plan should be operating as if ERISA does not apply, even if it technically does not. A nonprofit may find to its surprise that the non-ERISA umbrella has a lot of holes in it.

One Bad Apple

You can say that all's well that ends well, and in that spirit, fiduciaries of retirement plans might take heart in a recent federal court ruling in the case of *Pfeil v. State Street Bank*—that is, if several years of costly litigation can be ignored.

The ball bounced several ways as the convoluted case made its way through the courts since 2009, when General Motors employees sued State Street Bank, the fiduciary for the retirement plans. The employees were angry that they had been allowed to continue investing in their own company's stock at a time when the troubled behemoth was heading for bankruptcy.

Ironically, the investments in question were part of a company ESOP, or employee stock ownership plan. By definition, ESOPs are designed to invest primarily in company stock. They are not meant to diversify across a wide variety of securities. The GM employees did not have to invest in the ESOP. They could have chosen from a menu of investment options, and they had the discretion to change their allocation on any business day.

As GM struggled, the ESOP had been bleeding money. Nonetheless, State Street continued to include GM stock in the list of options until November of 2008 and did not eliminate GM stock until March 2009. The employees sued shortly thereafter, claiming that the fiduciary had acted imprudently under ERISA regulations. The lawsuit said that State Street should have sold the stock the previous summer when GM announced its restructuring.

The case was dismissed in 2010 in US District Court, which ruled that State Street's decisions to buy and keep the stock should be presumed to be prudent. Various federal circuit courts had ruled since 1995 that an ESOP fiduciary, unless it seriously abused its discretion, was presumed to be acting prudently if it remained invested in the company.

The employees appealed, and in 2012 the Sixth Circuit Court reversed the decision and sent the case back to district court for summary judgment. Before doing so, however, it issued its opinion on the matter, which read, in part:

> The district court focused on the fact that plan participants had the power to reallocate their funds among a variety of options, only one of which was the General Motors Common Stock Fund. A fiduciary cannot avoid liability for offering imprudent investments merely by including them alongside a larger menu of prudent investment options.

> Much as one bad apple spoils the bunch, the fiduciary's designation of a single imprudent investment offered as part of an otherwise prudent menu of investment choices amounts to a breach of fiduciary duty . . .

With the case in front of it again, the district court for a second time ruled in favor of State Street in the summary judgment. Once again, it applied the principle that the fiduciary's prudence was presumed.

Meanwhile, however, another case had been making its way through the court system, and this one went all the way to the US Supreme Court. In 2014, the justices unanimously ruled, in the case of *Fifth Third Bancorp v. Dudenhoeffer*, that ESOP fiduciaries were not entitled to the presumption of prudence. At the same time, however, the justices issued clear guidance to the lower courts: they nonetheless should carefully consider whether such ERISA claims against fiduciaries were plausible.

Encouraged by the Dudenhoeffer decision, the GM employees appealed once again. The Sixth Circuit revisited the case in 2015. This time the panel ruled that even without a presumption of prudence, State Street still was not liable for its role as fiduciary of the General Motors ESOP. State Street's managers had discussed "scores of times" whether to continue the GM investments, the circuit court pointed out, adding that the independent fiduciary committee held more than forty meetings during the time in question to talk about whether to retain the GM stock.

The court pointed out that other investment experts and the fiduciaries of other pension plans had also decided to hold on to GM stock during the period in question. They concluded that under efficient-market theory, the current pricing of a stock reflects all that is currently knowable about its future prospects. The plaintiffs, the court said, had based their argument on hindsight, and there was no genuine issue. State Street's process in evaluating the GM stock was found to be prudent.

DON'T SPOIL THE BUNCH

What are we to make of it all? On the one hand, the Supreme Court has dashed the presumption that a fiduciary is acting prudently in such situations, but on the other hand it appears from this case that plaintiffs could have a tougher time showing that the process itself was imprudent. Even a victory can seem like little solace at the expense of so much time and trouble. State Street faced a protracted challenge, despite its many meetings and discussions on the proper course of action that it should take regarding GM stock. This was despite the fact that the case involved an ESOP, designed to offer the specific investments that the employees took to task.

The bottom line is this: fiduciary decisions are being challenged regularly in the wider world of retirement plans—and very often the plaintiffs are winning.

The *Pfeil v. State Street* case powerfully illustrates that a fiduciary can get in trouble by offering a single imprudent investment, even if it is part of a larger menu of good options. Even though State Street ultimately prevailed and the circuit court recently refused to rehear the case, the "one bad apple" analogy that it earlier had advanced still rings loudly. If you offer a bad investment selection, you can spoil the bunch—and invite litigation.

Nearly every plan that we review contains a few of those bad apples. The notion that you simply can offer a bunch of options because some of them are bound to be good could very well invite a challenge. The lesson should be clear: if you have a bad one in there, you need to fix it! It is essential that you monitor every single fund that you offer, and you need to do that on a regular basis.

Every time you consider whether to add a new fund or replace an old fund, it is your responsibility to make sure that it is worthy of your plan. You need to weigh all of the ramifications: Does it fit the investment policy statement for your retirement plan? What are the share classes that are available in the investments, and how do the prices compare? Are there restrictions that need to be considered?

Handling these matters in the right way does require a lot of additional work for the plan sponsor or investment committee. It is very rare for an investment committee to have the necessary level of expertise and resources. Few people have the time, inclination, or ability to go through the investment policy and analyze all the funds, choose the lower-cost share class, conduct regular reviews, and do everything else that supports a high-quality investment program. This calls for professional guidance. Almost every investment committee will need to hire a co-fiduciary to help with that analysis and with those decisions.

A TWO-SIDED BENEFIT

We recently began working with the sponsor of a 401(k) plan that was offering 148 investment options when we came on the scene. That certainly provided a lot of opportunities for a bad apple. Why were there so many choices on the menu? The plan menu selections had been provided by a nonfiduciary insurance broker who had chosen to offer all available investments rather than evaluate which ones were of quality.

I see that scenario quite often, particularly with sponsors who rely on nonfiduciary salespeople. Their sales process is often incongruent with the fiduciary process. Salespeople are repelled by that responsibility. The pitch goes something like this: "Let's just offer all the investments so we do not have to worry about selecting any specific funds—this lowers the liability, and we will be in compliance with section 404(c)." I see many CPAs make the same assumption and mistake. This sounds like good advice backed by some legal reference. Nothing, however, is further from the truth.

Looking at all those offerings through a fiduciary lens, we realized quickly that the *majority* of them were of low quality. We were able to winnow that long list to the twenty-five best funds, through a prudent research and data-analysis process. As a result, those twenty-five investment choices became the only ones offered on the menu. It was far less confusing for participants. Who wants to research dozens upon dozens of funds? The employees received the selection of higher-quality investment choices, and we set up a process to continually monitor the investments.

The benefit, in other words, was two-sided. The employer got a plan and a process that came into better ERISA compliance, and the participants got a plan of higher quality. That is what we strive to deliver. That is the dual goal. As a fiduciary, you want to stay out of trouble, certainly—but the end result of all your efforts should be a strong and attractive plan that will serve your employees well as they prepare for retirement.

CHAPTER THREE

Choosing the Investment Menu

Even for experienced investors, the financial marketplace can be a quagmire of complexity as they sort through a multitude of securities and ponder when to buy and when to sell and when to hold tight. If the challenge can boggle even the best, how can a typical employee be expected to choose well among the options in a 401(k) plan? Would those workers be more likely to make wise decisions if their plan gave them a wide variety of choices or a more limited menu?

That fundamental question—"Are large menus better than small menus?"—has been the focus of recent research, including a study published in 2011 by the Harvard Business School. The researchers, David Goldreich and Hanna Halaburda, pointed out that the prevailing belief was that larger menus, by their nature, would be better, even though most employees found smaller ones easier to grasp. The presumption was that fully informed employees would prefer a wider range of choices.

What the researchers discovered instead was that those who create the menu tend to offer more selections primarily because they lack sufficient expertise to narrow the choices. Those with greater ability tend to produce smaller menus for the employees. In short, the study found that a lot of investment options within a plan indicates that it is more likely to be lower in quality. The conclusion: smaller menus are better than larger menus.

A wiser design limits the offerings. We need to advance beyond the theory that if you offer a wide variety of investments, the package is bound to include some good ones that will balance out any bad ones that might slip into the mix. That turns out not to be the case. Less really is more, as the Harvard study and others have recently determined.

The research suggests that the choices tend to be of a higher quality when trustees take a more reasoned approach than just throwing a lot of funds into the plan. In my view, the studies highlight the pressing need to pay much more attention to those choices on the employees' menu. If you would like to read some of those studies, you can find them at our website, www.fiduciarywisdom.com.

CHOOSING THE INVESTMENT MENU

So what is the right number? How many investment selections should you offer in a retirement plan? In my experience, any number greater than twenty becomes less desirable, and whenever you add a fund beyond that limit, you are adding 10 percent to the confusion for plan participants.

The plans that we manage, therefore, will typically end up with about twenty funds. We understand and abide by the principle that fewer is better. We work hard to ensure that funds will be of greater quality. The goal is to provide a menu that is small enough for the participants to manage effectively while also including a healthy variety of investments to construct an efficient portfolio.

You are probably familiar with the Morningstar ratings of mutual funds. The funds are distributed among nine boxes, each representing a different asset class for equities. If you offered just one fund for each of those types, you would have nine selections on your menu to start. To be in compliance, you also would need to offer a bond fund, and you also might want to include a money market or guaranteed account. That brings you to twelve funds.

Now consider whether you will be adding some index funds to the mix or whether you want actively managed funds. If you agree with the philosophy that less is more, then you might not want to include nine index funds within your plan. Indexing is fine if you weigh the pros and cons. What I don't like about indexing is that it guarantees you 100 percent of the market risk, and it does not provide any way to reduce that. What I do like about indexing, however, is that it is inexpensive. Active management is a little more expensive than indexing, but in certain periods and slices of the market, active managers simply do a lot better than the index. True, managers who can beat the index can be hard to find, but I have been identifying active managers who provide high value for twenty years—so I know that they are out there.

The big debate continues regarding passive versus active investing, but the global fiduciary standard is that a plan sponsor should engage both. As a fiduciary, you will be wise to offer both index funds and actively managed funds. A well-designed retirement plan comes with a sturdy and diversified toolbox.

Let's say, then, that you decide to add five index funds and then include a few more types of bond funds. That brings you to a total of about twenty funds among the menu choices that you are offering to your employees. With that number, you have the flexibility to provide all of the asset classes that will be needed to build an effective portfolio, and you also will have active and passive funds within the plan.

Even if you narrow the selections to below twenty funds, however, you still are giving the employees a lot of investment choices. Unfortunately, most plan participants simply do not know what to pick. They may not have the skill or the interest required to build a portfolio. They likely have never heard of modern portfolio theory and would not be able to define asset allocation. And they probably do not have an investment advisor. So how are they going to figure out where they will be putting their money? The world of investing can be complicated and confusing.

As the plan sponsor or administrator, you are thinking about such matters as compliance and ERISA rules and what the regulators and the enforcers might have in mind. The plan participants, however, think of their 401(k) or 403(b) as simply an investment plan, which is really what it is. They are making a sacrifice today to put money into the program so that it will grow and they will be able to enjoy a better lifestyle. They generally are not giving much thought to the details of the plan document and what goes on behind the scenes. For them, the investments on their menu are the heart and lungs of the program.

Dealing with the particulars—such as creating the investment policy and an investment committee charter, and monitoring the plan—can be complex and challenging. Ultimately, someone has to decide what to include in the menu. With so much to consider, how can you choose an appropriate menu while staying in compliance with ERISA and your fiduciary duty?

The haphazard approach that many retirement plans took in earlier years is no longer acceptable, as the recent court decisions and regulatory changes have underscored. To get good results and to be in compliance, sponsors must pay much more attention to every aspect of the process.

THE INVESTMENT POLICY STATEMENT

The process starts with a document called the investment policy statement (IPS). The statement lays out the criteria that investments must meet to be included in the plan. Who will make the decisions to include or exclude fund choices? How often will the investments be reviewed? What about outside advisors? If you are hiring somebody else to make these decisions, the IPS should say who is responsible for them.

Clarity is essential in setting those investment goals and policies, but plan sponsors often find the drafting of the IPS to be a daunting task. They can easily get lost. I strongly recommend getting professional help with this responsibility from a consultant or an attorney who specializes in ERISA matters.

In essence, the IPS is a set of directions, and the investment committee has to live by them, so they should be comprehensive. Unfortunately, the statements tend to be generic, with such pronouncements as: "Investments should be in the top quarter of their peer group for the past five years." Although that is better than saying nothing about quality, the best approach is to be more specific, although not to the point of losing flexibility.

Those sort of generic statements often come from vendors, and they do not always provide objective analysis or recommendations. They often suggest plans that are just sign-off-and-put-it-on-a-shelf. That is an easy approach for the vendor. It is not what is best for the participants, though—and that is paramount.

Of key importance in drafting the IPS is that it be linked to the process for analyzing the funds. For example, the IPS should not merely state: "We will only buy five-star Morningstar funds." That has been proven to be a poor investment strategy.[1] A good IPS includes such fiduciary particulars as comparison of rates of return, market upside and downside capture, analysis of fees, and asset-allocation strategy of particular funds. The IPS should have conditions for when to place funds on a watch list and when to remove an underperforming fund. You should not just make up your own system for choosing what gets on the menu. Use a proven system that incorporates the fiduciary components to evaluate investment choices. These systems tend not to be easily available, and it may be a bit of work to find a good system. Whatever system you choose to use, make sure that the plan sponsor and fiduciaries understand it and that any hired co-fiduciary advisor is using a quality analytic.

Do not limit your options too much. For example, you should not specify the number of funds that you will have in your plan. Instead, you could state the general asset classes that you will be including. You could say whether you will be offering both index funds and actively managed funds or whether you will include target-date funds (TDFs) and risk-based investment options.

---

1   Christopher B. Philips and Francis M. Kinniry Jr., "Mutual Fund Ratings and Future Performance," The Vanguard Group, Inc., June 2010, http://www.vanguard.com/pdf/icrwmf.pdf.

Just be sure that the IPS remains flexible. If it is too specific, you might end up with only a few investment choices that meet the criteria you are setting forth. You need to strike the right balance when writing the IPS so that it is not too generic and not too specific. Write it in a way that will be evergreen.

This important document should be required reading for everybody on the investment committee. You need to know precisely what the IPS says because it governs the investment quality of the plan. And there is another simple and compelling reason: you will be judged upon it.

It is crucial yet optional. You do not *have* to create an IPS. No law anywhere requires that you draft this document—so you should require it of yourself! When the DOL decides to audit a retirement plan, they typically will ask for two things up front. First, they will ask for the plan document. And then they will want to see the investment policy statement.

Some clients have told me that their "plan advisor" actually recommended that they not create an IPS. "Don't even draft one," they were told, "because then you will have to stick to it. You will be creating rules that you have to implement. You're better off if you just go blind and pick some investments."

Here is what can happen if you decide to go blind. One day, you find yourself testifying in court, trying to defend yourself against a claim that you blew your fiduciary duty. It seems that some of your employees feel that they deserve to be made whole.

"Please explain your rationale for choosing to include this investment in your 401(k)," an attorney for the plaintiffs asks you.

"Well, we liked it."

"Yes, you liked it. We do understand that," the lawyer says, displaying a practiced look of incredulity. "But just what do you mean? What did you like about it? How did you go about comparing it to other investments? Do you have any universal standards?"

That is what the IPS provides for you—a set of universal standards that you use for selecting investments. If anyone questions your selections, you will need to establish that you abided by such standards. When creating your IPS, think procedurally, and document the steps that you took. How did you go about it? Who made which decisions? How often did you agree to review the policy, and did you document that decision?

You can amend your IPS as needed, and it is not difficult to do so. In working with our clients, we typically examine the statement in an annual review. If that review shows the IPS to be aligned with the current plan, no amendments will be necessary. If you do need to make a change, we will help you. For example, we reviewed an IPS that was silent on the subject of hiring an investment advisor. We recommended that the plan specify that the committee would hire an advisor who would have the responsibility of selecting investments. The amendment did two things: It helped to eliminate confusion over whether the committee had the authority to hire the advisor, and it also helped to transfer the fiduciaries' liability.

DEFAULT INVESTMENTS

Invariably, some employees will be plan participants in name only. They do not take an active role in managing their money, and therefore they are at risk of not getting the most from their investments. Perhaps they need some education about how to make wise investment choices. Perhaps they have been automatically enrolled in the plan and do not have the time or temperament to check out their opportunities. They may not even feel motivated to choose any of the investment options—so then what do you do?

The Pension Protection Act of 2006 addressed this problem by creating the QDIA, or qualified default investment alternative. The regulations, issued by the DOL, allow plan trustees to make investment decisions for participants who do not make them for themselves.

You must approach this responsibility very seriously. Whenever you are making a decision for a participant, it must be a good one. The standards require that when you provide a QDIA, the participant's money must be invested either in a life-cycle or TDF, a balanced fund, or some type of professionally managed account.

The regulations require that the QDIA be diversified to minimize the risk of large losses. It may not invest contributions directly into employer securities. In addition, the QDIA must not impose any financial penalties, and it must not restrict the participant or beneficiary from transferring the money into any of the alternatives offered in the retirement plan. The investment company or manager must be registered under the Investment Company Act of 1940, which typically will be the case for all of your mutual funds.

When an investment committee makes QDIA decisions, too often it does not really discuss them, but it should—and it should keep notes of that discussion. Why did you choose the type of QDIA that you offer? You need to pay attention to the nature of your QDIA and monitor it, reviewing it periodically in light of any changes to the investment menu. Very often, we see QDIAs that consist exclusively of TDFs. I believe that can be a problem. Let's take a look at why.

TARGET-DATE RETIREMENT FUNDS

To help make things simpler for plan participants—and to make money for themselves—the big mutual funds came up with the idea years ago of creating target-date retirement funds or TDFs. The plan participant chooses a fund that will coordinate with the year that he or she expects to retire. The fund is managed with that particular year in mind. Usually, the asset-allocation strategy becomes more conservative as the target date for retirement approaches.

To the participant, the concept of TDFs seems simple. Just figure out the year when you will be retiring, choose the appropriate fund, and you are done. Set it and forget it. You need never touch it again.

To investment companies, "never touch it again" translates to tons of profit. Nonetheless, these funds should be watched closely—but it is difficult to figure out what is inside them and how the assets are allocated. They are not standardized. The fees can vary significantly both in amount and in type. By definition, a TDF only considers your age, without taking into account how much risk you are willing to tolerate. Two participants with the same birth year could have very different risk tolerances, and a TDF ignores that critical factor.

If you were giving advice to your beloved grandmother, would you tell her to get involved in such a thing? Would you tell her to invest in something that you do not really understand because you think it is right for her based upon her age—and that she should never look at it again? Maybe not. And yet when the investment company representatives talk to participants at an enrollment meeting, they say, "Just figure out the day you will retire, choose that number in the fund, and you never have to do anything else."

It sounds so easy. That is why these funds have accumulated such a large amount of assets—and that is why I believe that TDFs are rarely appropriate for a QDIA. Some plans are set up that way for the sake of simplicity. My concern is that no one is thoroughly examining the TDFs.

I am not alone in my caution regarding TDFs. Fiduciaries need to think twice before putting them on the investment menu. The DOL is looking at them, too. In fact, it has issued the following guidance for plan fiduciaries:

- Establish a process for comparing and selecting TDFs.

- Establish a process for the periodic review of selected TDFs.

- Understand the fund's investments and asset classes and how these will change over time.

- Review the fund's fees and investment expenses.

- Inquire about whether a custom or nonproprietary TDF would be a better fit for your plan.

- Develop effective employee communications.

- Take advantage of information sources to evaluate the TDF and any recommendations to select it.

- Document the process.

If you have TDFs in your plan, it is time for a frank discussion with whomever is providing them to you. Ask what those funds do exactly, why they were selected, and specifically why they are considered appropriate for your participants. And document that conversation.

I believe that TDFs are bound to become the focus of lawsuits. Consider what happened to some investors who had these types of funds when the market crashed in 2008. If they had chosen a retirement target of 2010, they might have assumed that they were safe—because, after all, they were only two years from retirement. Many participants were shocked to find out that 80 percent of their assets were invested in the stock market—only two years from retirement. Shockingly, many lost over 30 percent of their money. It caught them by surprise—and anything in a retirement plan that comes as a surprise can also become a liability. Whenever a participant says, "I didn't know that I could lose," you can expect that trouble lies ahead.

To further complicate the TDF issue, studies conducted by Aon Hewitt and Financial Engines revealed that when participants combine a TDF with other funds in the menu, the overall return can suffer. Plan participants, concerned about choosing the wrong fund, tend to want to spread out the risk, and they believe that they can accomplish that by keeping their money in more than one spot. However, the study found that the returns for participants who used both TDFs and other funds were lower than expected, with greater risk. They actually reduced their returns by 2.44 percent, the research showed. I often have heard people complain about the 1 percent they pay in fees inside their plan. This study reinforces that poor investment decisions are far more damaging to returns than fees. You can read the study on our website, www.fiduciarywisdom.com.

That points to a major problem both in investor education and in menu construction. If you are offering TDFs, they need to be an all-in choice. The plan should include a restriction prohibiting the use of a TDF in conjunction with other funds. Participants who choose the TDF should use it for 100 percent of their assets. The plan fiduciaries need to create rules that help the participants make better investment choices.

A RISK-BASED SOLUTION

Plan participants can make better choices than a TDF. Generally, they are quite capable of choosing for themselves from among different risk categories. They have the experience and self-awareness to know whether they are conservative, moderate, or growth-oriented. Sometimes that changes, of course. When the news is filled with economic woe, for example, people tend to feel worried and turn toward a more conservative approach. Still, they know their fundamental mind-set.

We therefore promote the concept of a risk-based investment solution. Using the investment choices on the menu, portfolios can be designed in advance for conservative people, for moderate people, and for growth people. In the plans that we manage, about 80 percent of the participants will use the tool of the predesigned portfolios. What that tells me is that they are pretty accurate at assessing their own comfort levels of risk and that they prefer a "do it for me" approach.

"Raise your hand if you are a conservative person," I sometimes ask people when giving presentations. Some people raise their hands. "Raise your hand if you're a growth person, you understand the markets, and you're comfortable with the ups and downs, but you want your money to grow." Some people raise their hands. Then I will say, "All right, raise your hand if you're in the middle," and all the others raise their hands.

They do not hesitate. They instantly know where they are on the risk yardstick. It is an intuitive response, and I believe that it is accurate for them. They will abide by an appropriate allocation. They will not be bouncing in and out of the market, worried about their money. Their stability is what promotes success. In an investment program, what drives the returns is time in the market to let the economy grow and expand.

You can help participants to engage in risk-based investing in a variety of ways. You can offer those basic predesigned portfolios. You can provide them with a questionnaire that will give them a risk score upon which they can base an allocation. And whenever participants change their mind and their outlook—whether they wish to pursue growth or to play it safer—it is easy for them to make the change. In my experience, few will move from one allocation to another, and "trading the allocation" is very rare. You have provided them, however, with the high-quality tools for flexibility in a changing economy and a changing world.

CHAPTER FOUR

Are You a Fiduciary?

The retirement plan industry had been watching *Tibble v. Edison International* intently as the case worked its way through the legal system. Employees of the utility claimed their savings had suffered because of fiduciary irresponsibility, and they were making a federal case of it—all the way to the US Supreme Court.

Specifically, the employees, represented by Glenn Tibble, argued that Edison had recklessly managed the company 401(k) plan by favoring higher-cost mutual funds over ones with lower expenses. The retail-class funds were far more expensive than comparable institutional-class funds, the employees said, and Edison should have been monitoring and eliminating investment choices not in their best interest.

The district and circuit courts, however, ruled that the employees had filed the case too late to collect damages on much of their claim, pointing to a six-year statute of limitations under ERISA. The employees were awarded only $370,732 in damages for excessive fees and lost earnings from three retail funds placed in the 401(k) within that period. The other funds in question had been part of the 401(k) for longer than that. At the time of the litigation, the 401(k) was valued at $3.8 billion.

Edison wasn't denying its duty to monitor and review, but it maintained that it needed to do so only upon a significant change in the plan, and the lower courts had agreed with that position. When the case reached the Supreme Court in 2015, however, the justices unanimously ruled that the six-year statute of limitations did not apply in the way that it was being presented.

The responsibility to monitor is continuous and ongoing, the justices said, and fiduciaries must consider all plan investments at regular intervals and get rid of the bad ones. They pointed out that trust law often is cited in cases of ERISA fiduciary responsibility: "Under trust law, a trustee has a continuing duty to monitor trust investments and remove imprudent ones. This continuing duty exists separate and apart from the trustee's duty to exercise prudence in selecting investments at the outset."

In other words, the justices were saying that whenever plan fiduciaries do a review, they in effect are resetting the clock on the statute. The question is not whether the offending fund was first offered within the previous six years. The question is whether it continued to cause a breach within those six years as the fiduciaries continued to monitor it.

The Supreme Court decision was a wake-up call for plan sponsors—but not so much because of the emphasis on monitoring the investments. Most plans should have prudent monitoring processes in place. More significant was this: the justices, in stripping away the boundaries of the six-year statute, in effect were expanding the right of employees to sue over fiduciary issues.

The justices did not rule, however, on the scope of Edison's fiduciary duties in the case. Instead, they vacated the earlier ruling and punted the case back to circuit court for additional consideration.

And that is where this tale takes another twist. About a year after the Supreme Court decision, the circuit court in April 2016 again sided with the company. The circuit court ruled that the employees never had presented an argument that Edison had that ongoing duty to monitor. They had focused only on the specific changes to the plan—and what they had failed to bring up earlier, they could not bring up now, the court said. The employees had forfeited their opportunity to take that position. Case closed—at least as far as the circuit court was concerned.

THE *TIBBLE* EFFECT

What we have here is another example of ping-pong litigation that ultimately has resulted in the doors opening wider for challenges to retirement plan fiduciaries. In the end, Edison prevailed apparently. And also, apparently, plan participants will find it easier to sue fiduciaries.

The federal courts have been seeing a new surge of class-action lawsuits, most claiming excessive fees. The plaintiffs' arguments appear to be getting increasingly sophisticated as they and their lawyers have learned through experience what works to produce settlements or rulings in their favor.

The *Tibble* case reinforces the concept of an ongoing responsibility to regularly monitor all of the investments offered on the retirement plan menu. If one of your selections is going to be the XYZ fund from the ABC mutual fund company, then the next question that you need to ask is this: "What is the cheapest share class in which we can purchase this fund?"

That is a consideration that can get you pretty far into the weeds. The answer will depend upon a number of factors. It will depend, for example, upon the company from which you are buying the fund. It will depend upon the size of the retirement plan. It will depend upon some of the restrictions within the mutual fund. It will depend upon the relationship that your advisor has with those mutual funds. Sometimes an advisor will be able to get exemptions for cheaper shares.

Those are just some of the factors—but nonetheless, the courts clearly have been saying that if the fees are excessive just because you did not pay attention or failed to ask the right questions necessary to get cheaper funds, you are responsible for a fiduciary breach.

The *Tibble* case ultimately should contribute to making retirement plans better, with more careful management. The lessons that surfaced during the case likely will be reflected in how sponsors operate their plans.

- They will be creating better systems to monitor the investments and to document that monitoring.

- They will limit the number of investments that need to be monitored—and, as we saw in chapter 3 with the Harvard Business School study, that's not a bad thing.

- They will review plan fees more regularly. With our clients, we conduct those reviews annually.

- They will increasingly transfer liability for fund selection to co-fiduciary investment managers, as permitted under ERISA law. We will take a closer look at that provision in chapter 7, where we will examine how to build the right team.

- They will wisely cease to participate in behind-the-scenes payments known in the industry as revenue sharing. This is indirect compensation, drawn from the investments, that goes to plan providers and advisors. Plaintiffs often characterize those payments as hidden and excessive fees. We will take a closer look at revenue sharing in chapter 7 as well.

WHO IS A FIDUCIARY?

You may be wondering who would want to be a fiduciary under such circumstances. Certainly it is a serious responsibility and a crucial role in the financial world, but it comes with an increasing risk of liability as fiduciaries find themselves in the fishbowl of public scrutiny. The reality is that plan sponsors assume a fiduciary role when their plan starts operating. Thankfully, they are willing to accept this responsibility in order to provide their employees with a critical benefit that helps prepare employees for retirement.

The lesson, illustrated not only by the *Tibble* case but by a flood of litigation nationwide, is that plan sponsors and administrators need to intimately understand the role of fiduciaries and what is expected of them. That understanding is essential if you are to get your plan into compliance and provide the best results for your participants.

The fiduciary concept is an old one that is rooted in English common law. A fiduciary is someone who has been entrusted with someone else's money, such as for safekeeping or investment, with the expectation of protection, assistance, loyalty, and sound counsel.

The fiduciary, in other words, has control of that money and must do only what is right with it. When you act as a fiduciary, you are taking on the major responsibility of making decisions that will serve only the best interest of others, without conflict or ulterior motive. It is a position of deep trust.

Who actually is a fiduciary in a retirement plan? That elemental question is a good place to start because we often find a great deal of confusion as to who wears that hat. The ERISA definition of fiduciary includes these fundamental types:

- **named fiduciary**: one who is specifically identified in the plan documents by position or by actual name

- **functional fiduciary**: one who has any discretionary authority or control or who can make decisions regarding the plan or its assets, regardless of official title or position

In addition, ERISA explains the role of "co-fiduciary," one who accepts a fiduciary status to help manage the plan—for example, a designated investment manager. Having an investment manager who is a co-fiduciary, however, does not necessarily excuse the plan fiduciaries, named or otherwise, from the responsibilities of their status. ERISA does provide for transfer of liability to a "3(38) co-fiduciary," as we will see in chapter 7.

Every 401(k) and 403(b) plan needs to identify who the plan fiduciaries are, and those fiduciaries need to know their responsibilities. In a 401(k) plan, the company owner typically is the sponsor. A business manager or human resources director typically is the plan administrator, who also could be making fiduciary decisions, depending on how the program operates. In a 403(b) plan, however, the fiduciary responsibility may be spread out more. At a nonprofit, for example, the responsibility falls on anyone who is on the board of directors or the finance committee, even if those people are volunteers who do not actually work for the organization. In chapter 6, we will take a closer look at fiduciary roles at nonprofits.

You will note from those descriptions that you can be a fiduciary even if you are not designated in writing as one. You might think that as a volunteer on a board you are just trying to help out, but you still may have that fiduciary responsibility.

In short, you are a fiduciary if you are making any decisions regarding the 401(k) or the 403(b) plan that affect the participants. You automatically are a fiduciary—a *named* fiduciary—if you are the company owner who is operating a retirement plan for your employees.

Some of the people who are involved with the management and control of a plan will be in the category of functional fiduciary because of the actions they perform. They could be making those decisions as an employee, or they could be making them as a volunteer member of the board of a nonprofit organization. If your answer is yes to any of the following questions, for example, you are a fiduciary:

- Do you make decisions about the plan service providers?

- Do you review and select the investments—or should you be doing so?

- Do you review the plan fees—or should you be doing so?

Examples of fiduciary-level decisions include structuring the plan, choosing any of its vendors, selecting the investment menu, and approving loans or hardship withdrawals. Those decisions clearly will have a direct influence on the participants, and a variety of people in an organization could be handling such duties. They might include administrators, finance committee members, board members, and business managers.

However, if all you do is process the payroll deduction or handle similar chores, you probably are not a fiduciary. Generally, there is an administrative exemption. Service providers such as actuaries, investment companies that offer only the plan platform, accountants, third-party administrators (TPAs), and consultants who provide no investment advice generally are not considered to be fiduciaries of the retirement plan.

STANDARDS OF CONDUCT

Fiduciaries must meet high standards of conduct under ERISA, although the law itself does not sharply define those standards. Over the years, however, DOL guidance and case law have helped to refine those definitions. And when those standards are breached, it is clear under ERISA that plan participants can seek appropriate remedies. If you fall short of your fiduciary duties, the participants of the retirement plan may make a claim of fiduciary breach that could end up in court. Litigation awards can be paid from assets of the plan sponsor or, in some cases, the personal assets of the fiduciaries.

As a fiduciary, you have a wide range of responsibilities and concerns, but they come down to two primary functions: you need to do the right thing for the participants in the retirement plan, and you need to protect the organization and yourself against liability. To do that effectively, you need to understand those standards of conduct under ERISA.

First and foremost, as a fiduciary you must act solely in the best interest of the plan participants and of their beneficiaries within the plan. I suggest to my clients that they become obsessive about that concept of "solely in the best interest."

As you go about making plan decisions, you also have to make sure that you are carrying out your duties in a prudent manner. Not only do you need to follow the terms of the plan document, but you also have a responsibility to diversify the plan assets and to minimize the risk of large losses. You need to be prudent in the way that you allow the participants in the plan to invest their assets.

If you think you might avoid all that fiduciary responsibility and liability by simply not looking at those plan fees or investments, be forewarned: that will not get you off the hook. If you are the one who could be making those changes, then you are a fiduciary—and you also are one who is ignoring his duty. Fiduciaries get in trouble not just by taking improper actions but by failing to take action at all. Neglect is also a breach of fiduciary responsibility. In fact, a fiduciary can be held liable even if he or she is aware of another's breach and makes no reasonable effort to remedy it. If you hold your tongue, you could be considered complicit, even if you resign and step away.

In one recent court case, the plan sponsor hired an investment manager to provide an analysis of the assets in the plan. The investment manager told the sponsor what he believed would be the best procedure for diversifying the assets and minimizing the risks. The sponsor, however, did not follow the advice, and the court ruled that failure to do so was in itself a fiduciary breach. It's not prudent to ignore your own expert, the court said.

The fiduciary responsibility is considered the highest standard of care known to the law, whether or not you are aware that you have that status. As applied by ERISA to retirement plan fiduciaries, the primary duties are these:

- duty of loyalty, or acting in the plan participants' best interest

- duty of prudence, or acting with the skill or diligence of a prudent person, and seeking the help of prudent experts

- duty of diversification, allowing plan participants to adequately diversify their portfolios and minimize the risks of a major loss

- duty to pay only reasonable expenses, by evaluating all plan costs and compensations to ensure that they are appropriate for the services provided

- duty to follow the plan document, complying with it in the administration of the retirement plan

Those responsibilities imply the duty to monitor—that is, formally review the service providers and other fiduciaries on a regular and ongoing basis. The penalties for breaching those duties can be severe, and they apply whether you caused the breach yourself, failed to take action upon learning of another fiduciary's breach, or failed to monitor another fiduciary when required. Depending upon the nature of the violation or fiduciary failure, you could face

- personal liability to restore any losses to the plan;

- a 15 percent excise tax on the value of any amount used for your own benefit;

- court action requiring equitable relief;

- a civil penalty of 20 percent of the amount recovered from your breach;

- criminal sanctions; or

- disqualification from ever serving as an ERISA fiduciary again.

Your fiduciary role is all about your actions and your decisions and how they affect the retirement plan. Let's say that participants in your plan claim that you did not handle their funds in a prudent manner, and the regulators start looking into your management of the plan. They will look at the things that you did. What were your actions? What decisions did you make at the time? What information did you use when you made those decisions? Did you keep a record of your decision-making process? I often say that ERISA is a verb—your *actions* are what matter.

Whether or not you are held liable will be determined by an analysis of your actions. ERISA tells you the standards that it wants you to meet, but it does not tell you exactly what to do—and it is that "what to do" part where most institutions really need help. They need professional assistance to make sure that they are operating a top-notch retirement plan that is fully in compliance with the changing regulations.

PROHIBITED TRANSACTIONS

Not only do you need to be fully aware of what you should do, but you need to steer clear of things that you should never do. ERISA contains a "prohibited transactions" rule that specifies certain activities as off-limits because of their potential for insider abuse. *To engage in such transactions is the worst thing that a fiduciary can do.* In essence, you must never pull money out of the plan for any reason other than expenses that are necessary to operate the plan and that you can fully justify as permissible, necessary, and reasonable. As an extreme example: taking your colleagues on a cruise, paid from plan assets, is not the right venue or method for educating them about the plan.

Let's say that you find an accountant who will charge you $1,000 to prepare your Form 5500 to file with the IRS. Another accountant would charge you $3,000. If you hire the latter for exactly the same service, you have overpaid. Unless you can show good reason, you are obligated to use the cheaper service. You therefore need to understand and carefully compare the expenses and what you get for them. Not only must you know the service provider's fee, but you must also understand the scope of services that you are getting for that fee. If you are facing a complex scenario that clearly calls for a higher fee, then that fee would be necessary and appropriate for the operation of the plan. Finding that right balance between costs and services is a universal problem that we see regularly when dealing with both 401(k) and 403(b) plans. We will take a closer look at fee analysis in chapter 7.

In general, the ERISA provisions ban certain transactions with "parties in interest." The intent is to prevent the fiduciaries from improper dealings with people who could have an influence over the assets of the plan. The ERISA rule aims to avoid self-dealing and conflicts of interest. A fiduciary must not allow the plan to engage in the following activities with such a person:

- a sale, exchange, or leasing of property

- a loan or other extension of credit

- a provision of goods, services, or facilities

- a transfer or use of the income or the assets of the plan

- an acquisition of employer securities or real property, except under certain conditions

To prevent self-dealing and conflicts, ERISA prohibits any transactions involving the plan that could benefit either the fiduciary or any person or entity in which the fiduciary has a financial interest. In addition, the fiduciary may not represent or take action on behalf of anyone whose interests are adverse to the plan.

Prohibited transactions can lead to fines and lawsuits, and the IRS could even move to disqualify the plan. If your plan is disqualified, all of your employees' tax-deferred contributions must go back to them as taxable income, and they will not be eligible to roll over distributions to an IRA or to another employer's retirement plan.[2] The distributions generally will be taxable in the year that the participants receive them. The money that you contributed to the plan as an employer match—and for which you took a deduction—will come back to you to be recaptured as taxable income.

Such an extreme penalty does not happen very often—but it is possible with egregious failures, and everyone involved with the plan suffers severe consequences. When it has happened, it has not necessarily resulted from a prohibited transaction. Generally, plans have been disqualified for one of the following violations:

- failure to adopt plan amendments required by the IRS, or taking too long to do so

- failure to follow the terms of the plan document

- failure to meet or correct the various IRS requirements regarding who benefits from the plan and how[3]

---

2   Deschutes Investment Consulting, LLC, "Plan Disqualification: Top 10 Errors & Consequences, Consequences of Plan Disqualification," (2016), http://www. deschutesinvestment.com/plan-disqualification-top-10-errors-consequences/.
3   Bill Freedman and Ben Wells, "10 Reasons that Disqualify Your Plan," Dinsmore & Shohl, LLP, http://www.dinsmore.com/files/Publication/db74b694-3d9b-4b19-9508-

CONFLICTS OF INTEREST

Let's say that you are responsible for managing your company's 401(k) plan, and your brother-in-law works for a financial company. It seems that every Thanksgiving, when the family gets together, he pulls you aside to say, "You know, I'm thinking you should just let me manage that retirement plan. We're a big company, and we do this all the time. I know that I can do a great job for you. And hey, you have to pay someone to manage all that money, so why not keep it in the family?"

Your brother-in-law slaps you on the shoulder and reminds you of how family members have been there for one another through the years. For a while you try to change the subject, but eventually you relent. You hire him to manage the plan. "Just make sure you do a good job," you tell him.

The big problem is this: if anyone decides to challenge the management of the plan, it might not matter much whether he did a good job. The fact that he is your brother-in-law is likely to become the issue. Imagine the case as it might be presented in court. Was your decision to hire a member of your family based solely in the best interests of the participants? A plaintiff would be seeking to establish an undue influence that broke the rules of fiduciary responsibility.

Perhaps, when you are called to testify, you will be able to explain exactly how, in your fiduciary process, you did uphold that duty. First, you made sure that your brother-in-law really is an expert and that he has the experience to manage your plan well. You understand and benchmarked his fees against those charged by the experts at a lot of similar companies. If you really did your homework—and

bbebd38ebfaa/Presentation/PublicationAttachment/c8e785da-f152-47d2-bc3b-cc32e02897a5/10-Reasons-plans-fail-halfsheet-download.pdf.

documented that you did it—and if you can demonstrate that your brother-in-law really was the best choice for the job, then you will have protection from liability.

That scenario might seem to be an obvious conflict of interest. You might think that most company presidents would recognize that they would be begging for trouble if they hired their brothers-in-law to advise the retirement plan. Unfortunately, we see cases like that a lot.

IT GETS PERSONAL

Here's one good reason why you will want to do your utmost to protect yourself against liability: it gets personal. You cannot hide behind a corporate veil.

As a fiduciary or a board or committee member, not only can you be found personally liable for losses, but you could also face DOL penalties. You can be assessed civil penalties equal to 20 percent of the amount recovered. Let's say you made an error that caused $100,000 in damage to the plan. The participants sue, and they win their case. Your personal assets could be taken to repay them. On top of that, the DOL could add that 20 percent "shame tax."

Many companies have filed for bankruptcy in recent years—and often, the fiduciaries mistakenly believe that their obligations to the retirement plan can be discharged along with the debts. Let me say it plainly: it does not work that way. As failing companies desperately try to keep their doors open, they occasionally will commingle retirement plan assets with the company operating funds. Sometimes the contributions collected from employees do not find their way into the retirement plan. That is a serious violation of both ERISA and the bankruptcy code. Such wrongdoing will not be erased by bankruptcy proceedings.

In the past, fiduciaries could sometimes skirt their duties, but consumer protection legislation has put an end to bankrupt employers abandoning their retirement plans. The DOL is empowered by ERISA to recover any missing employee contributions. If the employer has no assets and has closed its doors, the department goes after the personal assets of those who were the fiduciaries to make good on the losses. It can put a lien on the fiduciary's personal property, garnish future income, or even go after the fiduciary's own 401(k) account—and this might happen years after the company closes.

That should be reason enough for fiduciaries to make sure that the company, no matter how close it gets to the edge, never for a moment even thinks about mixing the plan assets with the operating funds. No matter how tough the going gets, even if it ends in bankruptcy, they still will be held to their fiduciary duty.

As you can see, this is not a position to accept lightly. Fiduciaries need to understand what they are doing. Many do not. The good news is that all these fiduciary responsibilities are manageable, and the results make the plan better. Through a quality governance process, the liabilities can be mitigated. You can proudly operate an excellent retirement plan, knowing that you have taken the proper steps to address the full range of concerns.

Designing Your Plan Document

For years, the plastic box had been shuffled from office to office and from shelf to shelf. The nonprofit institution had lacked a regular business manager for a while, and so nobody paid much attention to the box, which contained the retirement plan document.

Meanwhile, trying to react responsibly to a tough economy, the nonprofit's board had approved a reduction in the matching contribution to the plan. The institution cut the percentage of the contribution in half, taking care to make the change to everyone's employment agreement.

Inside that plastic box, however, the plan document continued to offer the match at the original percentage. Nobody thought to change it. Several years passed, until one day a sharp accountant blew the dust off the box, examined the document, and delivered the bad news: "We have a problem here . . ."

According to that governing document, the nonprofit should have contributed over the years about $300,000 more than it actually had. As fiduciaries, what were they to do now? Their duty, after all, was to look out for the best interests of the plan's participants.

That's when I got the call. Our initial role was to provide an assessment of the plan's investment quality—what it was doing right and what it was doing wrong. The board understood that an analysis would be a good idea in light of the frequent turnover of business managers. Upon the discovery that the plan document was outdated, we stepped back while the nonprofit hired an ERISA attorney to deal with those immediate problems. Once that issue was cleared up, we then came in to improve the governance and quality issues. The nonprofit ultimately was able to take care of that mess in a way that was compliant with ERISA, but the effort took a lot of time and money.

THE BIBLE OF YOUR PLAN

The plan document is the design by which your retirement program operates, whether it is a 401(k) for a company or a 403(b) for a nonprofit organization. It must spell out, completely and accurately, all of the basics, and the law requires that you put those details in writing.

You can think of that document as the bible for the plan. It is the rulebook that establishes procedures and requirements for the sponsor, the fiduciaries, and the participants. It is the operating manual by which you run the plan for the sole benefit of the participants.

The plan document must clearly state who is eligible to participate in the plan. For example, it must specify how long an employee needs to work at the organization before he or she can participate. The document also must spell out the benefits, such as how much the employer's matching contribution will be. It must explain the investment options, clarify how the money will be distributed, and describe any optional provisions such as a catch-up program or automatic enrollment. In addition, it must incorporate provisions that are required by the IRS and the DOL.

The plan document can be either individually designed or pre-approved by the IRS. Individually designed documents are created by a lawyer to meet the specific needs of an employer who requires more flexibility in the provisions. The preapproved documents come in two forms: "prototype" plans and "volume-submitter" plans, with the latter offering somewhat more flexibility.

Most retirement plan documents are one of the preapproved types. The plan sponsor may select some features and reject others. Any of those features will be compliant and will satisfy the requirements for the plan's special tax treatment. The IRS sends the company a routine letter saying that it has determined the document to be legal and approved.

The process of setting up a plan is fairly straightforward, although until recently it has been more challenging for nonprofit institutions. In the for-profit world of the 401(k), the company contacts a TPA to talk about the features desired for the plan. The TPA then can prepare one of those preapproved documents that already has the blessings of the IRS.

However, in the 403(b) world, the situation has been different. The nonprofits were formerly not able to use a pre-blessed plan document, and they did not have a clear way to submit their plans to the IRS to get them approved. This has been changing—the IRS has opened a channel for nonprofits to submit them and has recently begun accepting the prototype documents. For years, though, the situation generated a lot of confusion, resulting in many nonprofits having anemic plan documents that now require attention.

REVIEWING AND AMENDING THE PLAN

When an organization decides to install a retirement plan, what often happens is this. A vendor comes in and presents a three-ring binder with a load of information. The officers thumb through it, ask a few questions, look at one another and nod—and then put the binder on a shelf. The officers go about their busy day, and somebody from payroll sends in the money every week. Nobody gives the plan document a second thought, or at least it doesn't seem to rise very high on the priority list.

You need a formal review process. The list of things that you should check regularly is relatively short, but it will go a long way toward making sure that you are doing your part and doing it right. It is all too easy to get out of compliance with the complex and changing regulations. Never do you want your retirement plan committee to have to hear the words, "Uh-oh, there's been a mistake." You need to follow the plan document precisely and attend immediately to any updates.

Not only is it a good idea to attend to those updates, but it is also the law! With the continuing legal and regulatory changes, sponsors must amend and restate the plan document so that it remains in compliance with the IRS. Changes may be required to update the plan provisions if the employer wants to make an adjustment in benefits. If your plan is audited by the IRS or by the DOL, they will be examining the document to make sure that it is up to date.

Many of those changes are relatively minor and can be accomplished through amendments, but periodically the IRS requires an entire rewrite, or "restatement," of the plan due to the number and complexity of the changes. Generally, depending upon your type of plan document, you can expect that every six years you will need to rewrite it and submit it for review and approval. The latest round of required updates incorporated provisions from the comprehensive reform legislation of the Pension Protection Act of 2006.

If you miss a deadline for a restatement, the consequence potentially could be the disqualification of your retirement plan. It's a nightmare for both the employees, who could face immediate taxation on their plan assets, and for the employer, who besides penalties could be denied the tax deductions. Fortunately, the IRS does offer a correction program, under which you can pay a sanction and submit an updated plan. If you report your error and take the appropriate steps to make it right, that sanction is likely to be far lower than if the IRS discovers a document error upon an audit or from a complaint by a participant.

Many of the institutions with whom we work need to make changes to their plan document. Either it needs to be updated, or it is missing important information. For example, the document might be silent on how many loans a participant can take out from his or her account. John has one loan, Mary has three, Jerry has four—and the human resources department has a headache trying to sort them all out. The fiduciaries need to decide whether to alter the policy to specify that participants can have only one loan at a time.

Because you are responsible for adopting and maintaining the plan document, you must be diligent about those regular reviews so that you can deal promptly with any concerns and challenges that might arise. If you have a plan document that is not current, or if you are not abiding by the provisions in the plan document, you could be facing a significant problem. The DOL and the IRS do not look kindly upon that.

You should not be operating your 401(k) or 403(b) in any way that is not specified in the plan document. Unless you know what the plan document says, however, you will not be able to follow it. If you are a fiduciary, you need to read it through and thoroughly understand its provisions. Yes, you may be facing the prospect of digesting a thick document with a lot of checkboxes and charts, but you need to know the rules. In fact, you can consider that to be your plan's number-one rule: read it and understand it.

THE SUMMARY PLAN DESCRIPTION

To get an overview of the important elements of the plan document, a good place to start is the summary plan description that accompanies it. This will be prepared by the TPA who created the plan. Even if the summary plan description is all that you take the time to read and comprehend, you will be well ahead of those who just put the plan document on a shelf and never bother to open it at all.

The summary plan description usually is a wrap-up of one to three pages that describes the basic plan provisions and benefits in understandable language, free of the legalese that characterizes the plan document. You do not need to file it with the DOL, but you must provide a copy upon request, so be sure that it reflects the same amendments that you make to the plan document.

The summary plan description includes such details as:

- the name and type of plan

- eligibility requirements

- description of benefits and when participants have a right to them

- procedures for claiming benefits and how to dispute the denial of claims

- explanation of contributions to the plan and how the amount is calculated

- statement on whether the plan is pursuant to a collective-bargaining agreement

- provisions for terminating the plan

- statement on whether the plan is covered by termination insurance from the Pension Benefit Guaranty Corporation

- statement of participants' rights under ERISA

ERISA requires that participants and beneficiaries receive a copy of the summary plan description of their rights, benefits, and responsibilities, as well as a summary of modifications that have been made to the plan. You do not, however, need to distribute a copy of the plan document itself to participants unless they request it.

A PLAN OBJECTIVE STATEMENT

A plan objective statement, or mission statement, is another key element of your retirement plan's design. It is not an ERISA requirement, and it is not a governing document, but I believe it is crucial to put in writing your organization's set of goals and objectives for the retirement plan. It serves as the paradigm by which you will make decisions regarding the plan.

This should be a clear statement, separate from the plan document, that clarifies why you are establishing the plan and what you are hoping to achieve, such as attracting and keeping valuable employees and helping them to build their retirement portfolios. Your decisions then should be in keeping with that stated mission. Let's say, for example, that you decide that your mission is to have a high-quality plan that will maximize your employees' ability to save for retirement. If you make that pronouncement, the features within the plan should support it.

It would hardly be in keeping with that statement of objective, for example, if the plan included provisions requiring new employees to put in an entire year before they were eligible to participate, or if you provided no employer matching contribution, or if the plan offered only one investment choice. Those limitations might indicate something other than the spirit of maximizing.

If you want your mission statement to be consistent with what you actually are doing within your retirement plan, then you should carefully draft that statement during the design and documentation phase. Your goal, after all, is to create a savings and investment program by which your employees one day will be able to retire successfully. You are offering the means to fulfill an honorable mission—and that is quite a serious responsibility.

CHAPTER SIX

New Rules for Nonprofits

"Could you take a look at our retirement plan?" a top executive of a nonprofit asked when she approached us a few years ago. She had some questions. And when we took that look, we had even more questions.

The executive had been volunteering on the board of another nonprofit in Delaware whose retirement plan we had been rehabilitating. She had heard specific answers to our specific questions. It got her to wondering about her own nonprofit: If those questions had been directed to her, would she have been able to produce that information?

"I just want to make sure that our 403(b) is up to par and running the way that it should," she told us. "Something doesn't seem quite right." Once we started to investigate, we had to agree.

As is typical with nonprofits, her business office was understaffed, and the employees felt overworked. She told us that the plan seemed just too cumbersome to administer properly, and so we began what amounted to an X-ray of it to diagnose the issues. (This process grew into our Plan X-Ray service; you can learn more about it at www. fiduciarywisdom.com.)

We observed immediately that this was a plan with very low participation. Only about a third of the employees were contributing anything—and since the nonprofit was providing a match for those contributions, the employees were missing out on a lot of potential compensation.

Our biggest obstacle from the start was getting a comprehensive report on how the plan assets were invested—what I call the *homeostatic allocation*. We could not get a view of the balances. We were given a few statements, but they simply did not add up to the amount of assets that we had been told were in this plan of thirty-seven participants.

Nor could we get a Form 5500, which plan sponsors are required to submit annually under ERISA rules for reporting and disclosure. We could not find it online, although the form sometimes can be difficult to track that way. However, we did not get a hard copy when we asked for it, either. Clearly this was a plan that had been subject to ERISA from the start, based on its structure and on the fact that the employer was contributing funds. "Our CPA told us that we didn't need to file a Form 5500," we were eventually told, but their CPA was wrong.

As we asked more questions, we learned that a health insurance salesman had offered to help the nonprofit set up its retirement plan back in 2004. He was not a retirement plan expert. He simply called a mutual fund company and had it send out the application paperwork. Soon the mutual fund company then began setting up individual accounts for each participating employee, which is an old legacy structure for 403(b) retirement plans.

Eventually the plan grew to thirty-seven separate accounts. The payroll department was withdrawing the employees' contributions, adding the employer match, and carving the money up monthly into those individual accounts. The mutual fund company was mailing the statements to the account holders' home addresses. The nonprofit, in other words, was not able to track the overall assets itself.

After we eventually were able to assemble sufficient information, we found that about 60 percent of the assets were in a money market account. Much of the money that was transmitted to the mutual fund company was not even being invested. And we realized that every investment that the participants were making was subject to a sales charge. Upon each investment deposit, they were losing about 5 percent—an extremely high expense.

We then asked to see the plan document, required by ERISA. It details plan eligibility, benefits, and features. What we were given was simply the application forms to the mutual fund company. There was no real plan document.

We therefore were working with a nonprofit that had no plan document, that was filing no form 5500, and that was blind to what was happening to the investments. Major pieces were simply missing. There was no real monitoring of the plan at all. In a variety of ways, it fell short of a modern plan structure. The participants really did not understand how it worked. The low level of participation no doubt resulted from that confusion.

Embarking on a strategy to fix all those problems, we started with the plan document. We brought in a TPA to help us draft a document based on the way the nonprofit's plan actually was operating. The TPA designed the plan to reflect the match and to add other features.

After getting that squared away, we had to deal with the structure of the investments. We helped the nonprofit to understand why those individual accounts were basically precluding its fiduciary responsibilities under ERISA. Then we sought to determine the best alternatives for the plan assets. We worked with groups of plan participants, opening discussions on what they believed an ideal plan should look like, the features they would want, the appropriate size of the investment menu, and the types of help they would need.

Was this an active group that was interested in following the nuances of the market? We suspected not, given the high percentage of their contributions going into money markets. They seemed to be more the set-it-and-forget-it type of investors rather than the sort who would be hunkering over their computers to monitor the changes. Nonetheless, we wanted them to have appropriate tools in the plan for asset allocation and rebalancing.

We ultimately recommended an "open-architecture" style of retirement plan, a format that we will look at more closely in chapter 7. We felt that structure would include the most tools and features in a way that would be most conducive to the needs of both the participants and the sponsor. The nonprofit board was pleased with our recommendation and understood why these fixes were needed.

When we implemented the changes, we encouraged all the participants to consolidate their assets into the new investment structure, and most of them did so. They were comfortable with the new pooled approach and the open-architecture structure. They liked the tools that we made available to them, and they could clearly see that it was less expensive, since we were able to use institutional shares rather than the retail shares.

We also installed a monitoring and governance process so that the nonprofit and plan participants would have a much better idea how the investments were being selected. They could clearly see online, in one location, all of the plan assets. It was a far superior system than what the nonprofit had been doing, which basically was sending money into the mutual fund company and hoping that it got credited into the right accounts.

The results were even better than we could have expected. As we set up luncheons to educate the staff on the advantages of the new plan, participation increased from a third of the employees to two thirds. Their deposits in the plan went up by 25 percent, and their costs went down significantly. The surge in participation was primarily due to their new understanding of what was happening. They now felt that someone was watching out for them. The plan sponsor, too, was excited about the dramatic upgrade of services and benefits. The entire staff seemed appreciative of the efforts to fill them in on what was happening behind the scenes. They liked our role as fiduciary to the plan, helping to select and monitor the investments, because they did not feel they had the expertise to do it themselves.

This is an example of a plan that was able to rise, in the space of about fourteen months, from noncompliance, to become one that operates efficiently and speaks to the specific needs of both the employer and the employees. It is a plan that is now much easier for the business office to handle because it simply transmits a single deposit and the transaction is transparent. The view today is clear.

Many nonprofits need such help. Some people believe that if the nonprofit itself has passed an audit, the retirement plan must be in good shape, too. Not so. They are separate entities. The auditor of the nonprofit will be aware that the retirement plan exists but will not be examining its operational aspects. That is not what a nonprofit entity's auditor is paid to do.

Although most nonprofits these days have created plan documents and are filing their Form 5500, that is just the beginning of the new requirements that nonprofits have been facing in the last several years, as we will explore in this chapter. Every nonprofit will go through these changes in its own way. The steps will be similar, but the boards and committees will have different levels of expertise and differing priorities. They will progress at different speeds. Some will be keen on updating their plan as quickly as possible, while others will want to wait as they focus on other projects. It's the nature of the nonprofit world. The important thing is that they get onto the path and take those steps to make progress and come into compliance.

This particular nonprofit has become one of our greatest advocates. It realized what it had to do and rose to the challenge. Until we began working with it, it had no process for monitoring or keeping track of the new requirements that had taken effect since it created the plan. It had let its retirement plan go fallow, figuring that its situation had not changed.

That can happen so easily in the nonprofit world as time passes and no one brings these matters to the attention of the busy volunteers, whose expertise is elsewhere and whose attention is on other matters. On our website, www.fiduciarywisdom.com, you can read our white paper focusing on 403(b) issues.

THE NEW 403(B) ERA

As should be abundantly clear by now, the DOL and the IRS clearly have turned their focus in recent years to the 403(b) retirement plans with the intent of improving both compliance and operations. Unfortunately, many employers in the nonprofit world lack the time and expertise to adequately address these new requirements.

The "new" 403(b) era began in 2009, when major changes to IRS regulations took effect. In fact, they were the first significant changes to the 403(b) code in more than forty years. The regulations required nonprofits with retirement plans to do the following:

- Prepare a written plan document.

- File a Form 5500 annually, with a plan audit if required.

- Monitor limits on contributions to the plan.

- Comply with rules on loans to participants.

Those were among the immediate effects on nonprofits. The plan document, as we saw in the last chapter, is the nucleus for operations and for monitoring, and it has long been required of 401(k) plans. Only since the new regulations took effect, however, have the 403(b) plans needed to have one. For years, they were largely beneath the regulators' radar. Many operated without any written documents. We have found, moreover, that when nonprofits do have plan documents, they tend to be inaccurate. It is essential that this deficiency be remedied.

The influence of the new regulations on nonprofit organizations, however, goes deeper than getting documents in order. It involves restructuring how they administer and monitor their retirement plans so that they come into compliance and stay there. The regulatory changes apply now to most 403(b) plans, whose sponsors must be more careful than ever about how they manage them.

For nearly four decades before the new regulations, nonprofits had a fairly straightforward process for sponsoring a 403(b). They would sign up with a vendor, or several, to whom payroll would forward the contributions as the plan participants directed. Many administrative functions—such as loans, distributions, rollovers, and contribution limits—were handled at the vendor level.

The regulators, however, became increasingly concerned about compliance. The major issues that resulted in the new regulations were these:

- **Exceeding limits on contributions.** The company providing the investment product was supposed to monitor that limit, but often an employee's contributions went to more than one provider. Those companies typically were not working together to track the totals.

- **Violating limits on loan amounts.** Each vendor only monitored the amount of loans on its own books. Most plans therefore had little compliance with rules for loan repayment.

- **Investment quality and cost.** Most of the 403(b)s were structured as individual annuity contracts between the participant and investment company. Therefore, they lacked a plan-level economy of scale. Investment costs typically were higher than they were for 401(k) plans of similar size. Investment choices also were often proprietary and of low quality.

In issuing the new regulations, the regulators clearly followed the 401(k) model. The requirements are nearly identical. Plus, the DOL emphasized that the 403(b) plans also were subject to the same fiduciary standards. Under the new regulations, almost all 403(b) plans are subject to ERISA except for those offered by religious and governmental organizations. This is new territory, and many 403(b) sponsors are unfamiliar with their new fiduciary role.

A VOLUNTEER CULTURE

In many ways, a 403(b) retirement plan is very similar to the far more common 401(k) plan. They operate on par in almost every respect, including government oversight. In both, the employee contributes to a personal investment account. The employee's contribution may be matched, up to a defined level, by the employer. Both are "qualified" plans eligible for special tax treatment—namely, the deferral of income tax for the amount of the contributions until the account holder withdraws the money during retirement.

Today the duties of a fiduciary for either type of plan also are the same, under ERISA and the DOL rules. However, the nonprofit world and the for-profit world are culturally and financially different—and that in itself can present management issues for retirement plans.

In a business operating for profit, virtually everyone involved with the 401(k) plan is in some way on the payroll. As employees, those who have a fiduciary duty accept it as part of the job. At nonprofit organizations, however, volunteers often fill the positions on boards and committees—that is the major difference in the operation of 403(b) plan. The people in charge of it are often volunteers who are responsible for its operations but are not necessarily financially connected to the plan.

Nonprofits tend to operate with a lot of such volunteer work. Highly skilled professionals from the community—attorneys, financial advisors, accountants—serve as members of the board or the finance committees. That's where the governance of a plan typically takes place. The volunteers offer their time out of a sense of benevolence, attending meetings, perhaps bimonthly, where they make decisions and recommendations and vote on how the plan will operate.

Although the sponsors are trying to do the best for their employees, they can end up with significant compliance headaches. The volunteers may be highly knowledgeable and experienced in their own professions, but they are not experts on the complicated regulations and requirements of retirement plans. They are good citizens who have stepped forward to support a cause that they believe in, but they do not necessarily grasp the level of responsibility that they have taken on. They want to help the organization, but they may not realize that they could be considered to be fiduciaries.

I have seen cases where a problem arises with the retirement plan and a volunteer will say, incredulously, "What do you mean I'm responsible for this? I handed it off to somebody else." The task, perhaps, but not the fiduciary duty. As we saw in chapter 4, fiduciaries run the risk of exposing their personal assets to liability—and that is the case even for unpaid volunteers who do not understand the potential consequences of the role that they are playing.

To protect those valuable supporters from the risk of liability, nonprofit organizations must take measures to carefully manage the fiduciary process of their 403(b) plans. They need to specifically designate who will make plan decisions.

TURNOVER TROUBLES

Dealing with fiduciary responsibilities can be a particularly significant challenge for nonprofit organizations because they have a constant rotation of those volunteers on their board and committees. The turnover tends to be high on the governing board and the investment committee. Terms expire, people need to step down for one reason or another, and a new volunteer steps in. The members come and go. There may even be turmoil on the board that results in the sudden influx of a lot of new people, none of whom knows much about the previous members' plan governance decisions.

That high turnover of volunteers is a difficult problem for nonprofits, and a good advisor can go a long way toward providing a sense of continuity. The advisor can help to educate the newcomers, bringing them up to speed on the plan and explaining what their predecessors have accomplished. The records of all decisions, and when and why they were made, are highly valuable in that regard. If you can show the newcomers the last three years' worth of minutes, they will gain a good sense of how their colleagues have been operating the retirement plan. Those records are great educational tools for new members.

The records are also of major importance for helping to protect against liability if someone challenges the organization's fiduciary competence. Let's say the head of a school who made key fiduciary decisions years ago has long since stepped down and left town. Problems based on what that person did are just now arising. Those who were in any way involved in that decision-making could still be held personally accountable, even after all this time. Good records would help to ease that liability—but, unfortunately, records of just who voted on which decisions often are lacking.

That is one more reason that it is critical for nonprofits to clearly identify their fiduciaries and to make sure that all who fill that role fully understand how serious a responsibility they are undertaking. Anyone who volunteers to join a committee that manages the retirement plan should be apprised of what he or she is getting into. I have served on nonprofit boards and school boards and other organizations for decades, and I have seen liability issues come up and bite people who did not know that they were vulnerable. Nonprofits should take on the responsibility to provide guidance and training for their board members.

I believe that nonprofits should create a structure that insulates board members who do not volunteer to be fiduciaries. The board can do so by creating a retirement plan committee with a committee charter. That charter outlines the responsibilities for that committee and declares that those serving on it are fiduciaries during their time there. When they begin serving, they can sign a document to accept and acknowledge their fiduciary responsibility as of that date and until such time that they sign the second part of the document, where they will state that they no longer will be fiduciaries. In that way, empowered by the charter, committee members, in effect, can *sign in* and *sign out* as fiduciaries. Such a system clarifies and documents exactly which people were responsible for a decision and when.

TOWARD A MODERN STRUCTURE

Structurally, 401(k) plans have a leg up. For decades they have had an advantage because the fiduciaries can more easily make changes for the benefit of the participants. Historically, with 403(b) plans, that was not easy to do. The DOL has been clear that they should be run like the 401(k)s, but they were not set up that way.

Traditionally, 403(b) money was invested in fixed and variable annuities. This essentially left no way to update the investments. Monitoring seemed futile and was often given only minimal attention. Many nonprofits took a loose approach with their retirement plans in regulatory compliance and fiduciary roles. From a legal perspective, the plans should have been monitoring their investments carefully all along, but many were not.

Under the new rules, that has to change! The recent regulatory push has been a catalyst for changes that allow 403(b) plans to offer a greater range of investment options. Today, many plans have adopted a modern structure and can place contributions in a variety of mutual funds and other investment types. However, as they are offering more investment choices, the plan sponsors now must focus on more monitoring of those investments. The change is like owning a Ferrari: you get more power, but it requires more maintenance.

Historically, the 403(b) investment structure has been much different than that of the 401(k). All the contributions in a 401(k) plan flow into one big bucket that is invested on behalf of everyone in the plan. It is easy to make changes to the investment menu or other aspects of the plan because everyone's money is collected in one place.

In the 403(b) plans of the past, by contrast, each participant's money flowed into his or her own bucket. Each had a separate contract. It was virtually impossible to make changes, such as altering the investment lineup. As a result, the investments got stale. Sometimes, investments that were set up years earlier were never changed. Only the individual participants could update them, and some never again looked at the choices they made when they set up their account, perhaps a decade or two before. In fact, the vendor might never have offered additional choices. What's more, as the assets in the 403(b) grew through the years, the fee-pricing structure might never have been adjusted to reflect the economies of a larger plan.

Those traditional plans with individual contracts present a glaring problem for the fiduciaries: How can you prudently monitor the plan if one of the investments falls short of your standards? The separate contracts thwart your ability to manage the plan by adding or removing funds, and yet you still have fiduciary duties. Remember, "one bad apple spoils the bunch." You have to remove any bad ones.

There is no reason that a 403(b) cannot be set up like a 401(k) plan. It can, and it should. That structure allows you to attend to all of your fiduciary duties. Most 403(b) plans still need work to come into compliance, but the changeover is inevitable—the old structure is simply incompatible with the fiduciary requirement to monitor investments. As the 2009 regulations continue to push the nonprofit organizations toward the 401(k) standards, many of the 403(b) vendors are actively developing group contracts that give sponsors an array of investment choices with the ability to add or delete funds.

The 401(k) market has complied with ERISA for decades and is far more mature. It has more vendors and people with expertise, and, therefore, it is also a lot more competitive. Some organizations with a 403(b) plan find it worthwhile to switch over to a 401(k) instead, but I believe most should be cautious of that change. Most of our clients who have 403(b) plans choose to stay with them, particularly now that those plans have developed a better structure and more investment options.

Getting a 403(b) to where it needs to be takes commitment and time, but it is worth doing. What is needed will vary from plan to plan. The goal is to help the sponsor do everything necessary to bring the plan not only into compliance but to make it as effective and beneficial for the participants as possible.

MANAGING THE 403(B) IN THE NEW ERA

How can the sponsor of a 403(b) plan effectively manage those fiduciary responsibilities in this new era of ERISA regulation? In my experience as a plan advisor, sponsors find success when they take the following steps:

- They accept that they need to change how they manage the plan.

- They set up a retirement plan committee of fiduciaries who are qualified and committed, continuously updating that list on a fiduciary-acknowledgment document.

- They follow an investment policy statement and a prudent process to monitor investments.

- They understand all fees and the services received for them, and they establish that they are reasonable compared to alternatives.

- They document everything in a "fiduciary file," including committee minutes and attendance, what was evaluated and how, and decisions made and why. They keep updated copies of the plan documents, Form 5500, and IPS. The DOL, looking for a prudent process, recognizes only what has been documented.

To properly evaluate dozens upon dozens of investment choices is no easy task. Even organizations with large staffs find it difficult to establish and document a fiduciary management process. They may attract the needed talent, but then those people finish their board terms and move on. Nonprofits face the continuing challenge of identifying people with specific ERISA expertise who are willing to serve.

It is best to work with experts who will accept the role of co-fiduciary to the plan. The vendors of the old-style 403(b) plans with annuity contracts will never take on such a role. In fact, they are careful to establish that they are not fiduciaries. Many 403(b) plan sponsors add a co-fiduciary advisor to the team to support the committee. In that way the sponsor not only can share the fiduciary role but could also transfer liability to an ERISA 3(38) co-fiduciary. We will look more closely at that distinction in chapter 7.

The DOL is serious about its expectation that those in the 403(b) world should act in many ways as if they were in the 401(k) world. It has been hiring more people to expand its auditing capability. If you have not been paying attention to your plan, you could well face such an audit. You can expect a letter asking that you get dozens of items ready for the auditors. The vast majority of 403(b) plans, and many 401(k) plans, lack many of those items.

Paying adequate attention to your plan operations takes a lot of time and effort. When we work with organizations to bring their plans into alignment, they often ask, "Is this required?" The answer is yes; it is now. It is the right thing to do as a fiduciary, it is the right thing to do to protect against liability, and it is the right thing to do for the sake of the plan participants. In my view, the development of standards has reached the point where it should be considered a fiduciary breach if a deficient plan has been left fallow for a decade and the sponsors are intent on letting it remain that way.

Consider this an opportunity to dramatically improve the quality of your nonprofit's retirement plan while providing sound fiduciary management and protection from liability. In my experience, plan participants universally appreciate the improvements. At its core, ERISA seeks to help people save enough for retirement. By following the ERISA best practices, you can avoid the pitfalls as you strive for that harmony of purpose.

Building the Right Team

THE INVESTMENT COMMITTEE

When you are offering a 401(k) or 403(b) retirement program for your employees, the first question that you must address is who will be in charge of it. You may need to establish an investment committee and an operating charter for it that will identify those people and set forth their duties, responsibilities, and powers. The committee will be responsible for managing the investment menu, hiring service providers, and monitoring the plan as required by ERISA.

The investment committee does not need to be big. In fact, I recommend a relatively small committee of three to no more than seven people. You will need to make some real decisions. To avoid tie votes, you should have an odd number of members. Five is a good number—that way, if somebody cannot make it to a meeting, you still have a quorum and enough people to actually make some decisions.

To identify who will be on the committee, you might simply state that it will be the president and chief financial officer of the company and three others, perhaps one from human resources and two from the general staff. A nonprofit organization might establish a finance subcommittee for this purpose. You need to be more specific than just listing a large group, such as the entire board or management team.

As the plan sponsor, you should write the charter. A consultant can offer a draft as a starting point, but you will need to modify it because every institution operates differently. In writing the charter and appointing people to the investment committee, you are identifying the fiduciaries. That, of course, is a serious responsibility, and therefore each person should formally acknowledge it. As I described in chapter 6, they should sign a document acknowledging when they are taking on that fiduciary role and when they are stepping down from it. That piece of paper will be valuable whenever you need to establish—such as in a court of law—exactly who was responsible for which decisions and when. The document shows all the links in the chain and thereby protects everybody. A sample charter is available at www.fiduciarywisdom.com.

The investment committee members, as an essential part of their job, need to watch for red flags indicating a problem or a potential one. Here are some of the red flags that we most frequently see:

- There is no annual process or meeting to review the plan.

- None of the funds offered in the investment menu have been changed in more than two years.

- Most of the funds are proprietary and have the same name as the service provider—such as the ABC Insurance Company Fund.

- The mutual funds are retail class.

- The share classes in the funds are not the least expensive available from the platform.

- The total number of investments on the menu exceeds thirty.

Whenever any of those statements is true for your retirement plan, you need to take a careful look at it. We work with our clients to provide independent review as well as training and good management practices. We can help them in identifying the pieces necessary for running a good retirement plan and then selecting the right people to manage those pieces.

What to consider when developing a committee:

- Who in the organization has the time, ability, and desire to be on the committee?

- How large a committee do you need? Smaller is usually better.

- Do you want an employee representative or the advisor on the committee?

- What are the goals of the committee?

- How will you keep the charter evergreen?

- How will you document changes of members over time?

- How often should the committee meet?

Now that you have a committee and understand who is responsible for the development and selection of the service providers (vendors) that make the plan work, let's explore each element that makes up your plan.

WHO ARE THE PLAYERS?

Building your plan is like assembling a baseball team; it takes many parts to operate effectively. If you do not have a pitcher and a catcher, you can't start the game at all. The development of your infield is critical, as most balls are fielded in the infield. Your outfield becomes very important as you face opponents who are good hitters, and that outfield needs to know where to throw that ball so the runners can't steal extra bases on hits. In building your team to help operate your plan, you also need the critical positions, and they need to work together very well. Understanding the players of your plan is helpful because it identifies which functions are being performed by which vendor. Here is a graphic of a plan team:

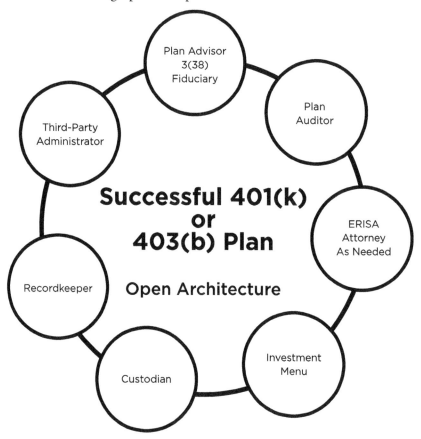

Let's take some time to explore each service provider and how they operate in your plan.

The Third-Party Administrator (TPA)

The third-party administrator often is the designer of the retirement plan, providing the plan documents to the sponsor. The TPA can handle many of its day-to-day operations and annual testing for compliance with governmental regulations. He or she may handle such tasks as preparing the benefit statements for participants and processing their loan paperwork, helping to process distributions, and preparing the annual forms and reports that the IRS requires.

TPA quality can vary, and TPAs typically do not act as fiduciaries, nor do they want that responsibility. The costs and services are rather standardized; they all do basically the same thing, and typically one is unlikely to be a lot more expensive than another. If your plan is more complex, or you have multiple plans or there is common ownership of multiple companies, then you may need a more specialized TPA that may in turn be more costly. In our experience, we have been able to lower costs using a higher-capacity TPA. Therefore, it may not hold true for all TPAs that greater complexity means higher fees.

What to ask TPAs:

- Inquire about their experience, and have them describe a typical client. Is that client like you?

- Get a full understanding of the services.

- Get a full understanding of the fees.

- Do they receive any revenue-sharing payments from other service providers? If so, quantify the payments.

- Will they use revenue-sharing payments as a credit against the fees?

- What is the plan-to-TPA employee ratio—the lower it is, the better the service.

The Plan Investment Advisor

Many organizations that offer a retirement plan to their employees do not have the in-house capacity and expertise to manage the investment menu. They are focused instead on their company's goals or products or services. Often the biggest challenge, beyond the basic plan operations, is how to select and monitor the investments. How do you competently offer a menu that is free of bad choices?

What if some of your original investment offerings have gone stale? Certain stock market sectors do better than others, and certain funds outperform others. Managers come and go. Have you reviewed how those dynamic and ongoing changes might affect the plan participants?

As we have seen, court cases have reinforced the fiduciary duty to regularly monitor investments. Unless your organization has somebody with the desire and expertise to monitor the plan well, it will be hard to meet that responsibility without assistance. To help them make the best selections, many sponsors therefore hire an investment advisor and manager. That person, or company, can function as a co-fiduciary under the basic definition in section 3(21) of ERISA.

By working with that advisor, you are proactively taking a step to show that you are trying to act prudently under the ERISA rules. In the case of a 3(21) fiduciary, the advisor recommends a list of investments, then steps back while the other plan fiduciaries vote yes or no on the recommendation. The advisor does not have the discretion to actually change the investment menu—only the sponsor can do that.

Many plan sponsors do not understand that important time when the 3(21) fiduciary steps aside and the plan sponsor approves the recommendation. Once they get into a relationship with an advisor, they just figure that he or she will handle everything. They do not recognize that they still are ultimately responsible. Adding the expert does show prudence—but it does not do anything to reduce the sponsor's level of liability in selecting investments.

Some record-keeping platforms, typically bundled, offer 3(21) services for a small fee. The investment menu is usually made up of a few lists of funds that are preselected for the sponsor to choose from. It is the action of selecting the menu that is a fiduciary action and an affirmative action to approve the investments. The 3(21) fiduciary is responsible for developing the list, and the plan fiduciaries approve that recommendation based on their analysis of the funds within the menu. We rarely see plan sponsors use 3(21) services.

Fortunately, ERISA offers a good way to both be prudent and lower sponsor liability, as we saw in the last chapter. This type of advisor, defined in section 3(38) of the ERISA regulations, operates in a much different capacity.

A 3(38) investment manager has the discretionary power to manage, acquire, and dispose of the assets of the plan. The advisor is typically registered as an investment advisor under the Investment Advisers Act of 1940. A 3(38) can also be a bank or an insurance company that is qualified to perform such services. Most importantly, 3(38) investment managers acknowledge a fiduciary position in the plan and allow the plan sponsor to transfer the liability to another fiduciary. They actively volunteer to take that higher level of responsibility.

A 3(38) investment manager can make life much easier for the plan fiduciaries. The manager has the authority to select and change investments without going to the board or finance committee for every change. In addition, the 3(38) manager's actions do not expose the fiduciaries to investment-selection or monitoring liability. If a 3(38) manager decides that ABC mutual fund has ceased to deliver as expected, he or she can replace it with XYZ mutual fund. The law specifically describes the "safe harbor" from investment selection: "No trustee shall be liable for the acts or omissions of such investment manager or managers or be under an obligation to invest or otherwise manage the assets for which that manager has responsibility."

A lot of investment advisors, however, operate under section 3(21), where the ultimate approval of the investment choices remains with the plan sponsors. If the sponsor wishes to transfer that investment selection and monitoring liability to someone else, that can only happen with a 3(38) manager. At a 2016 meeting with one of the largest insurance company platforms, we were told that they "never run into 3(38) advisors." I am confident that many plan sponsors are unaware of this critical difference in fiduciary classification.

Of course, as the plan sponsor, you cannot just transfer and ignore. You still are responsible under ERISA for monitoring all of your service providers. Just as you must regularly monitor and review what your service providers are doing for your plan, you need to regularly monitor and review the plan overall. This is a major fiduciary responsibility, and you must be sure that it is being met.

I believe you should be working with an advisor who is knowledgeable about retirement funds specifically—and who can demonstrate that experience. Your advisor must be properly licensed and registered, of course, but you also need to know, with absolute clarity, whether the advisor will be functioning as a 3(38) fiduciary or in the limited 3(21) role. Review the contract, or have an ERISA attorney review it, to be sure that you are getting the level of liability protection that the advisor is promising. If you were to be sued, you would not want any surprises. I believe that the 3(38) fiduciary structure is often the best solution for plan sponsors. At BCM we only act as 3(38) co-fiduciaries.

Because the advisor will be helping to develop the investment menu, you will want to know that person's investment style. Some like to work with target-date and lifestyle funds, others prefer index funds or exchange-traded funds, and some focus on actively managed investments. You should be looking for the right fit for your participants. The advisor also must be willing to work with you in carefully documenting how those investment choices are made and how participants are informed and educated about them. That documentation can be critical in fending off liability. The link between the advisor and the fund menu is a critical one that we will explore in detail under the heading of the *total fee concept*.

What to ask an advisor:

- What is your fiduciary capacity, 3(21) or 3(38)?

- What are the average fees of your recommended fund menu?

- Can you quantify the fees in detail?

- What are the details of the services included in the advisory agreement?

- How was the fund's menu developed?

- In reviewing the fees for each fund, what is the highest and lowest fee fund in the menu?

- How are fund-share classes selected and monitored?

- Ask for a sample copy of the usual documents provided in a plan review—do they suit your needs?

- How many clients have discontinued your services in the last two years?

The Recordkeeper

The basic function of the recordkeeper is to keep tabs on all the participants' accounts and who owns what in the plan. That is a crucial role in a 401(k) (and in modern 403(b) plans) because the investments from all the participants flow into a common pool. The recordkeeper tracks how much each person has contributed, which investment choices he or she has selected, the extent of the plan sponsor's match, and other details of the operations.

Recordkeepers also provide account statements and document the outstanding loans that participants have taken on their accounts. Today's recordkeepers almost always have Internet and telephone access for the participants so that they can initiate changes in investments and beneficiaries and use tools for retirement planning.

Your choice of a recordkeeper is very important because it will have much to do with the participant experience. The employees will be dealing with the recordkeeper more than anyone else as they check account statements, access the website, request forms, and so on. You therefore will want to find out how a potential recordkeeper will be handling those nuts and bolts.

The services that recordkeepers provide will vary significantly, so there is not an easy standard for comparison. For example, one may offer asset allocation services, and one may not. One may offer self-directed brokerage accounts, and one may not. One may have access to exchange-traded funds as well as mutual funds, and one may not.

Previously, we talked about completing a plan X-ray exercise and that evaluation of what is working well in a plan and what needs some attention ties directly with the selection of a recordkeeper. If you have been able to survey the plan participants and determine what service they would like, that will help to refine the criteria in selecting the recordkeeper.

Recordkeepers generally will charge either a flat fee, a basis-point fee, or some combination of both. You should enumerate the services offered and what you are paying for each—for example, if the recordkeeper also acts as a TPA, what does each function cost? It is important to get that breakdown.

What to ask a recordkeeper:

- Is there a sample tour of your participant website?
- Can you specifically identify all fees?
- Is any revenue sharing being paid to other service providers?
- What is the scope of investments available?
- Could you provide a sample participant statement for review?

The Custodian

The retirement plan custodian is a financial organization—often a trust company or insurance company—at which the assets of the plan are actually held. It also deals with necessary documentation and tax-reporting requirements for the plan and ensures adherence to IRS rules.

The custodian service often is bundled with the recordkeeper service. Most custodians will charge in a generally predictable range, usually a basis-point fee.

What to ask a custodian:

- What are the levels for insurance coverage (FDIC, SIPC)?

- Could you explain in full your fee agreement?

- Will transaction fees apply?

- Are statements easy to read?

- Do any payments come in the form of behind-the-scenes revenue sharing?

The Auditor

Generally, when the total number of eligible participants exceeds one hundred, federal law requires a retirement plan to be audited annually. If that is the case for your plan, you must hire an independent qualified public accountant for the task and file an audit report each year. If that report is inadequate or late, you could be assessed penalties.

Auditors tend to provide similar services and charge similar fees, but it is essential to work with one who is experienced. A common reason that reports are found to be deficient is that the auditor did not perform required tests. That can happen when the auditor is unfamiliar with retirement plan practices and the specialized auditing rules that apply.

The DOL, in its fourth study of plan-audit quality, reported in 2015 that 39 percent of the plan audits did not comply with professional standards. That percentage was an increase over previous years: 33 percent in 2004, 19 percent in 1997, and 23 percent in 1988.

The study looked at the number of retirement plan audits that firms had performed for 2011 and the percentage of audits found deficient. The DOL looked at four hundred audits, choosing the sample from among 7,330 firms. Of those, 95 percent did fewer than twenty-five plan audits.

This was what the study discovered:

Plans Audited	Deficient Audits
1–2	75.8%
3–5	68.4%
6–24	67.4%
25–99	41.5%
100–749	12.0%
750+	12.0%

Clearly, if you hire an auditor who has little experience, you are facing a high likelihood that your audit may be found deficient. Deficient audits could lead to penalties of up to $1,100 a day, plus the cost in time and resources to set things right.

You will note that even the firms performing the most plan audits still had a deficiency rate of 12 percent. I believe you will be best served if you select a firm with extensive experience. Not only will you be exercising fiduciary prudence, but you also will be avoiding the inconvenience, embarrassment, and potential penalties should the audit be deficient.

What to ask an auditor:

- How many audits does the firm complete?

- Has any audit been classified as deficient?

- What percentage of the firm revenue is from plan audits?

- How many employees work in the plan audit division?

- Will an auditor be available for questions from the plan sponsor or other service provider?

- How many hours of the sponsor's time is required to complete the audit?

The study is available for further review at our website, www. fiduciarywisdom.com.

The Investment Menu

As part of the construction of your plan, someone will have to select an investment menu for your participants to use. This menu selection can be completed by the committee, a co-fiduciary advisor, or it may come as a function of selecting all available investments offered by the recordkeeper—I don't recommend this, as has been discussed in the prior chapters.

The plan investments—technically known as your designated investment alternatives (DIAs)—are the pieces your participants focus on. The other service providers are behind the scenes to most of the participants. Employees talk about and research the investment menu more than any other aspect of the plan. When a plan is using standard mutual funds, participants usually research the funds online using their ticker symbol to identify the fund and explore the historical returns, fees, stock or bond holdings, rating services reports and the fund management.

If your plan uses an annuity format, the investment menu may consist of what are known as separate accounts. One of the best ways to determine if your plan uses separate accounts is the absence of a ticker symbol for the DIAs. A separate account is an insurance account that is submanaged by a fund or investment company but not registered as a mutual fund as indicated by a ticker symbol. A sample description for a separate account would be the XYZ Company Large Growth Fund. Separate accounts may contain extra fees, and plan fiduciaries need to designate particular attention to a concept known as revenue sharing that we will explore shortly.

HOW DO YOU ASSEMBLE THE TEAM?

In procuring retirement plan services, you can take one of two broad approaches. You can work with a single provider that "bundles" together services. As you can see in the following image, the bundled approach encompasses the TPA, recordkeeper, custodian, and investment menu under one service provider. The bundled approach has some benefits and some drawbacks.

Benefits:

- selection of a single company—less setup work

- may offer more services for small plans with under $2 million in assets

- single point of contact for sponsor and participants

BUNDLED SERVICES

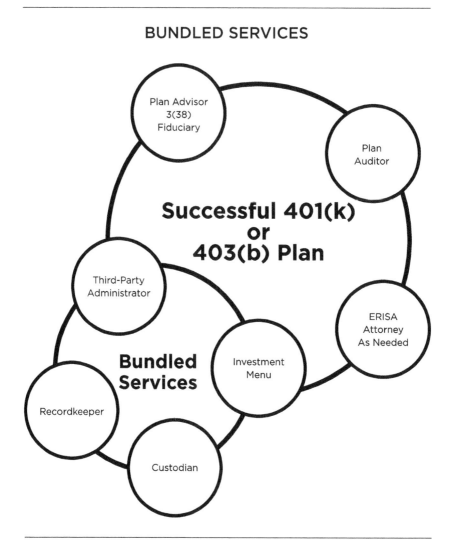

Drawbacks:

- higher fees

- difficult or impossible to change a service provider (just the custodian, for example)

- share class restrictions

- possible nonsupport of complex plan features

OPEN ARCHITECTURE

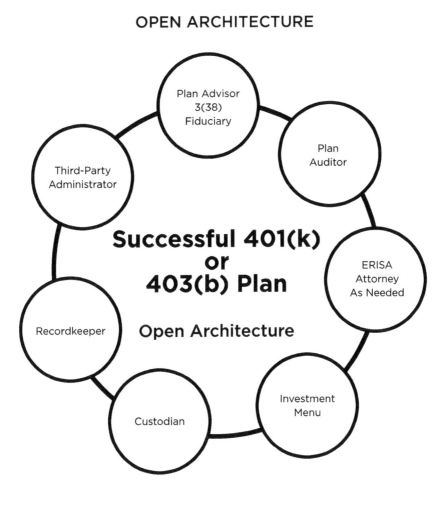

I have been advocating the open-architecture approach for many years, both for 401(k) plans and for 403(b) plans. It's a modular way to build your plan. You no longer are working with one investment or insurance company that handles all the details. If you want a different TPA or recordkeeper or investment advisor, for example, you can just replace that particular piece of the platform. If you are unhappy with a component, you do not have to start anew and reconstruct the whole plan, as you may have to do with bundled services.

Think of it this way: If your washing machine needed a new motor but the rest of it was functioning well, would it be best to replace the motor or to junk the whole thing and go shopping for a new one? Your retirement plan likewise has many moving parts, and not all of them are likely to malfunction at the same time. Why should you be junking the whole thing?

The open-architecture approach amounts to custom building a plan to best meet your needs and the needs of the participants. It is true that it does mean a bit more work in the beginning. Once the plan is built, you have to keep track of different vendors and monitor what they are doing for you. In the end, though, that is really not much more work than monitoring a lot of functions provided as a bundle by one company.

The key for the plan sponsor is to evaluate the overall cost as a sum of the expense of individual components. The fiduciaries need to understand what they are buying and whether the price is reasonable. What are the fees for the investment advisor, the TPA, and the recordkeeper? What are you getting for what you pay? In general, however, plan sponsors who opt for open architecture often find that fees are more transparent, customer service is better, and the level of expertise is high. They find that open-architecture vendors generally have access to better mutual funds, leading to an improvement in the investment choices.

Many companies are choosing open architecture to build a direct relationship with each service provider. You maintain control and can switch out those components. The relationships are yours, not the investment or insurance company's. You can choose the individual team members, and if one of them needs to go, you do not need to toss all of them out the door together.

With a proper investment policy statement and an astute advisor, open architecture should present no additional burden on the plan sponsor. The decisions about changing components of the plan, when necessary, should be relatively easy to make. This approach has been gaining steam because of its flexibility and because of its potential to reduce costs while adding more features to the plan.

COMPENSATING THOSE SERVICE PROVIDERS

Each service that is being provided to a plan will have some cost— nothing is free. Service providers get paid in a few ways: percentage of the plan assets, flat fee, per participant fee, or a combination of them all. Some fees are usually paid outside of plan assets and not assessed against the participants' accounts; the auditor is the most common of the employer direct-pay service providers. Obviously, the more fees the plan sponsor covers, the lower the fee drag for participants.

Fees are paid using one of two modes—direct debit and net-asset value (NAV). Direct debit is a simple charge against a participant's balance and should be enumerated on the participant's statement each quarter. NAV payment is a process that mutual funds (and separate accounts) go through where the management fee is deducted each day before the final valuation of each day's closing share price. This NAV process creates a feel for the participant that there is no fee, and these fees are not enumerated on the participant's statements. The NAV mode of charging fees is a way for service providers to hide fees.

MUTUAL FUND SHARE CLASSES

Mutual funds offer many share classes. A share class is a way for funds to offer multiple fee structures to investors. In the previous chapters you have seen the successful legal challenges to plans asserting that the sponsor was not using the proper share class. A good understanding of share class is very important for plan fiduciaries, as the courts have been very clear that sponsors need to strive to offer the participants the lowest-cost share class. Let's review an example.

Fund Name: American Funds American Balanced		
Share Class	Ticker	Prospectus Expense %
R6	RLBGX	0.29
R5	RLBFX	0.34
R4	RLBEX	0.63
R3	RLBCX	0.94
R2	RLBBX	1.39
R1	RLBAX	1.38

The American Funds American Balanced Fund is offered in many share-class formats. Each share class has a different total fee, but each share class may not be available to your plan. Share-class selection is based on a few factors:

- plan assets and annual deposits

- recordkeeper and custodian selected for the plan

- how each service provider is being paid its fee—revenue sharing

There is a large difference from the highest-cost fund, RLBAX, to the least expensive, RLBGX—1.09 percent. The fundamental management of the mutual fund does not change based on the share class, as the managers will select the same securities for each share class and the holding will usually be identical. The only variable that changes with share class is the fee charged against the participant's balance each day to establish the NAV.

REVENUE SHARING—COMPLEX BUT IMPORTANT

In this chapter, we have examined the components of your plan structure and who is on your team. Whether your services are bundled or you choose open architecture, understanding revenue sharing is a paramount skill.

Simply put, revenue sharing is the process by which many of those service providers often are paid through another vendor's fee agreement.

Here's an example of how revenue sharing might obscure a fee. Let's say you are a plan sponsor looking for recordkeeping services. One advisor tells you he can get recordkeeping from Provider A for twenty basis points. Another advisor tells you, "I can get you that service at zero cost." You might jump at the chance to pay nothing. The best value may look like Provider B—unless you realize that you must buy a more expensive share class. It's not really free, despite how the service is sold to you.

I manage a 403(b) plan with inexpensive institutional share classes, and I make sure that the sponsor and participants know that the cost for recordkeeping is twenty-three basis points. Others who are not as obsessive about fee disclosure could choose a much more expensive share class with a high 12b-1 fee and proclaim that there is no recordkeeping fee. It's there, though. It is just getting paid in a way that plan participants do not see.

Plan sponsors need to know that this happens. It amounts to a sales maneuver to get business and to make the provider look less expensive. Often, the plan sponsor does not know what is going on behind the scenes—don't be that person. I recommend that you become very persistent and force all vendors to disclose any revenue-sharing agreements with other vendors.

Let's look further into that America Balanced Fund to understand how each share class can affect revenue sharing.

SHARE CLASS EXAMPLE

Fund Name: American Funds American Balanced			
Share Class	Ticker	Prospectus Expense %	12b-1 Fee - Revenue Sharing
R6	RLBGX	0.29	0.00
R5	RLBFX	0.34	0.00
R4	RLBEX	0.63	0.25
R3	RLBCX	0.94	0.50
R2	RLBBX	1.39	0.75
R1	RLBAX	1.38	1.00

In the chart, you see six share classes (R1-R6) for the American Balanced Fund. One column is the total prospectus expense percentage—the actual fee for the fund as listed in the prospectus for each of the share classes. The other column is the 12b-1 fee. That is the revenue-sharing fee that is also charged within each share class. That 12b-1 fee can be paid to another service provider, such as the broker, the recordkeeper, the TPA, or the participants. In the most expensive R1 class, for example, the fee totals 138 basis points, or 1.38 percent. However, a full percentage point, or a hundred basis points, can go to pay someone else. The plan fiduciaries must know where those fees go and what service they are paying for.

In the R4 class for the American Balanced Fund, the fees total sixty-three basis points, but twenty-five of those, or a quarter of a percent, can go somewhere else. Every plan can be set up differently as to who gets a piece of that money. If it goes back to the participants, for example, their net expense in that share class would be thirty-eight basis points (sixty-three minus twenty-five). However, a retirement plan could instead be set up to pay the recordkeeper with those twenty-five basis points. That way you get the so-called free recordkeeper. That 12b-1 payment can be very hard to find on the participant fee-disclosure documents because the fee is deducted every day in figuring the fund's net-asset value (NAV) of total assets minus liabilities. In effect, the fee is hidden.

I am a big advocate for revenue sharing that goes back only to the participants. That keeps all the other service providers honest and forthright in disclosing their real costs. Your fees need to be open so that you can evaluate them. Both you and the participants must be aware of what is being paid. That is why, with the American Balanced Fund, I use only the R6 share class. It is the least-expensive class we can get for that fund, and no revenue sharing is involved at that level. There is no 12b-1 fee at all. The service providers are then forced to display their actual cost without the ability to "hide" fees from the participants.

THE TOTAL-FEE CONCEPT

I see many plan sponsors make mistakes when they do not standard-ize their fee analysis. I recommend the *total-fee concept*. This concept is one that is used by the DOL in its Plan Fee Disclosure Form. When you are evaluating any one service provider, you need to look at the impact on the total fees to the participant. Revenue sharing can distort the look of a fee proposal.

A good example that I work with daily is the plan-advisor proposal. Because you are hiring the investment advisor to help you develop and choose an investment menu, you need to understand that the advisor is also affecting the fees that are paid to the invest-ment/fund companies when they develop the fund's menu. Many times we see that plan sponsors do not link the advisor fee and the fees for the investment choices, *and this is a big mistake.*

Let's look at an example.

Plan sponsors who simply ask for the advisor fees alone and make a decision based on that single factor may very well make a decision that is counterproductive. Investment-management fees *must* be looked at comprehensively.

	Advisor Annual Fee	Average Fund Fees	Total Investment Cost
Advisor A	.45%	.25%	.70%
Advisor B	.25%	.65%	.90%
Advisor C	.05%	.92%	.97%

BUILDING THE RIGHT TEAM

As you can see, with all the focus on low fees, a plan sponsor may be tempted to hire Advisor B as the lower-cost solution. Advisor C is a 3(21) service that is offered through a bundled provider that looks very economical on the surface—but you know better now. If a plan sponsor does not ask or understand that advisor fees and fund fees are linked, they may make a big mistake—particularly if the advisor is getting a portion of the fund fees as revenue sharing. I advocate that every advisor-fee presentation must include a list of actual investments and the fees—or an average of the menu's fees. Sponsors should also ask for a share-class report showing the share class an advisor will be using for each fund. Ask for the fund ticker, and don't just accept an answer like, "We use institutional shares." You are a fiduciary; you need to look at the details.

I have analyzed many plan-advisor RFP requests, but I have never seen an RFP that includes a question linking the fund fees with the advisor fees. The reality is that it takes additional work to analyze the fund's costs and push them down as much as possible, and that work is valuable to participants as well as the plan sponsor. Total investment cost is an outstanding way for plan sponsors to flush out whether or not the advisor fee is reasonable for the services provided. This basic concept is the most missed aspect of plan management and advisor selection. Understanding the link between the advisor and fund fees can help you to directly improve the quality and lower the fees for participants.

ARE SERVICE PROVIDERS FIDUCIARIES?

The judicial trend supports the long-held view of service or "platform" providers, that they are not plan fiduciaries—and I agree with that position. The fiduciary responsibility lies squarely on the plan sponsor or on another who accepts that responsibility. Very often, sponsors presume that their provider—typically, an investment or insurance company—is a fiduciary. No, it is not, and the recent cases support that fact.

In the nonprofit 403(b) world, the plan sponsors believe, almost universally, that the large providers have this "fiduciary stuff" covered for them. I have even been in arguments with attorneys (not ERISA attorneys, however) over that matter. They cannot understand that the platform providers are not responsible for much at all. They do not accept fiduciary status.

What those court cases highlight is this: plan sponsors will benefit greatly from an independent advisor who will accept that fiduciary status. A quality advisor understands where the lines of responsibility are drawn—and you need that knowledge if you are to attain good governance and management.

Now you know both the players you need and some tricks to demystify the fees that the players charge. You can now count yourself far beyond the basic understanding of assembling a successful team to develop and oversee a stronger retirement program for your employees.

CHAPTER EIGHT

How Do You Stack Up?

PARTICIPANT FEES

"What about these fees?" a voice from the back of the room called out, somewhat louder than necessary. "They are just way out of line! How can we be expected to get anywhere if we have to swallow this kind of cost?"

I was conducting an enrollment program for a nonprofit organization at this time. That particular gentleman had become obsessed about fees. He had been doing online research and writing letters to the sponsor, complaining that the investment expenses were just too high.

In reality, the fees for that retirement plan were lower than the fees paid in plans across the country that were similar in respect to the amount of assets and number of participants. By that benchmark, they were fair and reasonable. Nonetheless, the letter writer was making the argument that the fees were too expensive compared to "what individuals could get on their own."

In that sense, he was correct. But an individual does not have to conduct compliance testing or follow fiduciary procedures. An individual does not have to comply with ERISA and hire a recordkeeper to track multiple accounts. The expense of operating even a small retirement plan is generally greater than the costs an individual will pay when handling his or her own investments.

However, retirement plans do have the advantage of economy of scale. Negotiating for lower fees can be easier for a plan worth $10 million than for an individual investor who has $10,000. As plans increase in size, they can become more competitive on fees. In some cases, the fees can be even less expensive because plans can access funds using institutional share class, to which individuals may not have access. For the previously mentioned gentleman, the plan size was not very large, so the costs were higher than an individual investor would be subject to.

What matters when analyzing fees is the quality of services you get for those fees—and whether they are reasonable. That is harder to quantify. Does the provider offer investment advice? What resources are on the recordkeeper's webpage? Does the advisor give a quarterly review or an annual one? Can participants contact the advisor? Is the TPA working with a complex plan structure or a simple one? Fees can be benchmarked. There are services that can help you do that, assessing exactly what you are getting and how much plans of similar size pay for such services.

Even after the implementation of the DOL-required fee disclosures, it can be very difficult for plan sponsors to fully evaluate and understand their plan fees. A good place to start is the DOL Fee Disclosure Worksheet.[4] This worksheet will help to quantify and categorize fees for your plan. It can be difficult even for a professional

---

4   U.S. Department of Labor, "ABC Plan, 401(k) Plan Fee Disclosure Form For Services Provided by XYZ Company, https://www.dol.gov/ebsa/pdf/401kfefm.pdf.

to fully itemize the fees for many service providers because they have decades of experience at hiding fees, as with the confusing behind-the-scenes revenue-sharing payments. The DOL worksheet helps to prompt a plan sponsor to ask the questions that help to expose the plan fees.

When plan sponsors attempt to quantify their plan fees, they should adopt an attitude of solving a mystery. Assume that plan vendors are hiding fees. Be both skeptical and very persistent. Plan sponsors should understand the plan fees in detail, as well as understand any and all revenue-sharing agreements. Use the total-fee concept.

In working with a nonprofit school, we went directly to the participants to ask what would help them the most—and they told us about the range of services they would find most useful. We reported back to the sponsor, suggesting vendors that could come close to meeting those criteria. That's the ideal way to set up your plan, customizing the vendors, costs, and services to the needs of the participants. If an additional service will assist plan participants to be more successful in saving for retirement, then add the service—even if it augments the fee slightly. With our experience in the industry, we know what similar plans pay for similar services, and so we can help gauge whether the fees are in line.

FAIR AND REASONABLE

Your fiduciary duty requires you to pay only *fair and reasonable expenses* for operating the plan. Let's take a closer look at what that means. In my experience, fair and reasonable expenses are often misunderstood, and the definition is getting out of control in the market.

One of a plan sponsor's main jobs is to make sure that the fees paid within the plan are reasonable for the services being provided. That requirement is universal, for both 401(k) and 403(b) plans. Regulatory changes have been turning a lot of attention to those fees, and along with that attention, there has been a lot of confusion.

Much of the confusion centers on the assertion that all fees should be as low as possible. And that is true—but that does not mean that the plan has to bring in the cheapest-possible vendors. In fact, the cheapest-possible vendor simply may not provide all the services that your participants need or that you want to provide to them. The true measure of fees is whether they are fair and reasonable for the extent and quality of the services provided.

Recent regulations have made it clear that the DOL is pushing for greater transparency in fees. The purpose is to help people make good decisions by providing a summary of the relevant information on fees. Two recent regulations in particular—404(a)(5) and 408(b)(2)—seek to enhance the disclosure of fees to promote better choices.

The first of those regulations, 404(a)(5), deals with fees at the participant level, and the second deals with plan-related fees charged by all service providers. Generally, the participants pay most of a plan's costs via investment-related expenses and direct contract charges, although they may get the impression that they pay no expenses at all. The regulation seeks to educate them about those costs, requiring sponsors to send a fee disclosure to them annually. The second regulation, 408(b)(2), aims to help fiduciaries assess whether fees that they pay to service providers are reasonable. If a vendor is paid out of the plan, it needs to disclose how much it gets and acknowledge if it is functioning as a fiduciary and what fiduciary type.

FEE-DISCLOSURE REGULATIONS

- ERISA 404(a)(5): This provision seeks to keep participants better informed about plan costs. It requires sponsors to send them annual fee disclosure statements.

- ERISA 408(b)(2): This provision seeks to help plan fiduciaries assess whether service providers are charging reasonable fees. The vendors must disclose how much they are paid out of the plan and their fiduciary type.

The emergence of such regulations highlights the importance of analyzing where your plan is today. If you do not know where you stand, you cannot know how to get to where you need to go. Failure to even consider this matter virtually amounts to a fiduciary breach in and of itself. I have found that many sponsors certainly want to manage their plans well but do not know how. The information that the recordkeeper or the mutual fund company provides is often confusing and hard to understand. It is difficult to know whether you are doing the right thing.

That is far from an unusual situation, and one solution is to find an independent person to analyze the plan for you. Look for a truly independent advisor who is not trying to sell you anything. A climate of sales is a problem in the retirement-planning space. A salesperson has an inherent conflict of interest when it comes to providing you with advice.

You are far better off paying a fee to an independent advisor to get a plan analysis that will be for your benefit. Look for someone who has clients whom you can cross-reference. Make sure that he or she does independent analysis as a full-time job and has experience evaluating retirement plans. You need that level of dedication and expertise. After all, you would not want to go to a doctor who practices for only a few hours a week.

AN X-RAY FOR YOUR PLAN

If you doubt whether your organization's retirement plan is all that it could be, or whether you are doing all that you could, you need to do something about it. That nagging feeling is a sign that you should be taking action. If you do not address it, you are not doing what is in the best interest of the participants.

You may wish to do a self-evaluation as a prelude to obtaining an independent view. That is a service that our clients have found helpful. Basically, you fill out a quick compliance quiz.

The quiz will self-grade and provide you with an analysis of plan compliance as well as suggestions. The free quiz can be found at www.fiduciarywisdom.com.

For a more comprehensive and custom evaluation, we have developed the Retirement Plan X-Ray, which you also can learn about at our website. We can provide a written report and analysis of your investments, governance, and ERISA compliance, along with recommendations on how to make your plan better via a scheduled review call with one of our retirement-plan advisors. It's an independent and comprehensive way to look at the underlying structure of a plan—to see whether anything is broken. In the appendix to this book, you will find a sample that illustrates how we conduct a Retirement Plan X-Ray.

In the X-Ray, we look carefully at the "homeostatic allocation," or HA. The HA reveals where the plan participants invest their assets based on the current investment menu and their level of education in portfolio construction. If, when we analyze a retirement plan, we see that half of the assets are in cash or a money market, we know the plan has a problem. The participants are not constructing their portfolios properly. We also might find that 50 percent of the plan's assets are in a single fixed account and 40 percent of the assets are in a single stock account. That indicates the participants need some help.

The X-Ray and HA can instantly reveal an education gap among your participants. We help our clients put tools in place to help their people make better choices. We customize the education to the workplace. We might suggest web-based retirement calculators to help participants project what they will have at retirement. We also can help them to build asset allocation models based on what they select as their acceptable level of risk. Each participant simply needs to determine whether he or she is a growth person, a conservative person, or a moderate person.

THE SUCCESS MATRIX

We help clients develop goals for their plan—a success matrix. We help them decide what has to happen in order for them to feel that their plan is operating successfully.

Every organization is different, of course. Some companies go from 20 percent participation in the plan to 80 percent participation. That's a big jump, a definite success. Others will go from 60 percent to 78 percent, which might seem to be less of a jump. But if a company has eight hundred employees and its enrollment rises from 60 percent to 78 percent, it is adding a lot of people to the plan—and clearly experiencing a success as well.

I encourage our clients to share that information with the participants. It is helpful to explain to them, "We have 42 percent participation. We want to be at 75 percent," or "Fifty-five percent of the people in the plan aren't getting the full match. We want 100 percent of the people in the plan to get the full match." By talking to the employees about their participation in the plan, the sponsor is communicating to them that the plan is an important part of their compensation and that the organization is paying attention to it.

I do not find it particularly helpful or accurate to benchmark a retirement plan's level of participation against others in the industry. The benchmark that really matters is how well your plan is achieving the goals that you have set for it. You need to identify the status of your plan today and decide where you want to go with it. Just because an industry average might tell you that participants should save 4.5 percent of their income, it does not necessarily mean that is what is right for your plan.

Take a close look at your own plan. What is the percentage of eligible employees who are deferring income? What is the average amount that they are deferring? How many people are getting 100 percent of your match, if you have one? Your TPA or your plan advisor and consultant can easily get that information for you. As a sponsor, you should always be trying to improve on your own success matrix. Track those numbers on an annual basis, and dedicate yourself to getting ever better.

PREVENTIVE MAINTENANCE

You can consider such examinations to be a form of preventive maintenance. When you watch your plan carefully, it inevitably will get better. When you regularly review what is going on with your plan, you will find problems much more quickly than if you let it lay fallow.

That is why your fiduciaries or investment committee should hold review meetings regularly, and those must amount to more than having lunch, then walking away telling yourself that you met. Regular meetings demonstrate that you are paying attention. Attendance matters. Business owners often are inclined to ask their staffs to handle such matters, but it is important that all the members attend.

Let me again emphasize the importance of documenting who was there and what was discussed. If you decide to hire your brother-in-law, the finance guy, as your plan advisor, for example, you had better be certain that the committee examined the entire situation and determined that he truly was the best choice. Further, it is very important that you demonstrate his value at each meeting through documentation and notes. Be absolutely sure that you are in compliance and without conflict of interest. You will also need to be able to clearly establish the details of why the committee felt hiring him added value to the monitoring process and the ultimate plan quality for the participants. You will need a record of how you reached that decision.

Your notes and records will be crucial if a problem should arise. ERISA's default position is: "What was the process you went through to make the decision, and how did you document it?" Keep that in mind for every decision. All the records of my clients' meetings—the attendance sheets, notes, minutes, and so on—go into an electronic fiduciary vault. They are on a cloud drive that we and the client, as well as the client's auditor, can access. If need be, we can grant authority for an investigator to look at those records, as well. The vault provides one central location for all the plan information. Some companies just keep all their information stuffed into a filing cabinet—definitely not the best approach. Neatness and organization convey a serious attitude and diligence to any examiner.

We complete investment analysis for our clients on a quarterly basis. Every three months, we evaluate every fund in every plan. Sometimes we find that their quality is improving, and sometimes we see they are starting to fumble. We are able to spot trends. Is that sector of the market just not doing so well that quarter? How does the investment compare to its peers? At least annually, however, we meet with plan sponsors and committees and provide a full fiduciary review, including evaluation of investment quality and allocation, compliance, plan amendments, fees and share classes, contracts with service providers, and the need for benchmarking.

CHAPTER NINE

Knowledge Is Power

Over the years, I have observed how thousands upon thousands of plan participants handle their investments, and I can tell you that 90 percent of them do not know what to do with their retirement money. They want help, they need help, but they do not know how to get it. The DOL is trying to close that gap.

As we saw in the last chapters—in our discussions on evaluating services and fees—the department has been pushing for better education to keep retirement plan investors better informed. Regulations require sponsors to disclose fees to them annually, and service providers also must disclose their fees.

These regulations resulted from studies showing that many employees believe that they pay nothing for the operation of their retirement plan. It is not hard to see why they would feel that way. Companies supplying retirement plans have long operated in an atmosphere of obfuscation, hiding their fees. They made it look as if their management was free, even as they were taking out big chunks of money.

Clearly, a retirement plan does not operate for free. A lot of work goes into maintaining it. All of those compliance efforts, for example, come at a cost. The providers know that, and the sponsors know that—and the emphasis now is on making sure that the participants know that as well.

EDUCATION AND ADVICE

Communications with participants must be clear and thorough if they are to get the most out of the retirement plan. They need to know what to do, when to do it, and all of the factors that they should be considering as they make their choices. After all, the whole idea is to give them a secure way to save for retirement. How are they to know whether their money is safe and being invested for their benefit? Do they know how to maximize their participation or even whether they qualify to contribute?

The more you can educate your plan participants, the better—and I believe that you should fill them in on what is going on behind the scenes. In our experience, employees will feel that the plan has a lot more value if they understand that the investments are being reviewed quarterly and that the fees also are under regular review. When they see the effort that you are putting into providing them with a high-quality plan, they will realize that this must be a matter of high importance and that they, too, should be involved.

That is why I have repeatedly emphasized in this book the importance of identifying your *goal* in establishing a retirement plan. When you know why you are providing one, it is much easier to develop programs to help the participants get educated. You need to understand the level of education that your people really need. For example, a workforce of engineers may require some different tools than a construction company. Remember, though, that even if you feel your engineers have a relatively sophisticated grasp of investing, not everyone in your company is an engineer. You must consider the needs of the entire staff.

A good way to gauge the sort of communications that participants need is to pay close attention to the basic questions they ask during enrollment meetings. What are you hearing? Are the questions relatively technical, asking about particular mutual funds and the fee levels? Or do you hear comments such as: "I don't know where to invest my money. I don't understand how this plan works. Why do I even need something like this?"

Clearly, the type of questions will help to indicate the directions you should take in educating your employees and the subjects that you should tackle. In my experience with many different plans and a wide variety of industries, the questions and concerns are different in every case. No education program will be quite the same as another. In general, I have found that 403(b) plan participants have not received as much education as those in 401(k) plans. That is not to say that 401(k) participants operate at a higher level; it simply reflects that they have been used to the flow of information. Since the PPA of 2006 required more of 403(b) plans, today they are trying to catch up with twenty years of 401(k) discussions. 403(b) participants must take a bigger jump, but ultimately, the process is the same: start with the goal, then educate the participants.

BASIC PLAN ADVICE

As a sponsor, you do need to be somewhat cautious about the advice that you give. Consider whether you are giving generic advice about the plan itself and the investments within it or whether you are giving specific advice for a participant.

Listen to the question. Let's say a participant asks, "I'm not sure what investments to use. Can you help me understand them more so I can build a portfolio?" That's asking for generic investment advice about the plan. Providing explanations and answering questions about how the plan and the investments function can and should be done. The employees need to understand the features of the plan and when they will be eligible to participate. Some will want to know whether loans are allowed, how many, and the maximum amount. What services are available within the plan?

However, let's say a participant comes to you with this question: "I just refinanced my mortgage, and I don't know what to do with the money I'm saving. Should I put it in my retirement plan or buy some life insurance? Or should I put the money in my child's college-savings plan?" That is a specific question from a specific employee, and if you answer it, you are giving individual investment advice.

I always recommend that a plan sponsor *not* give individual investment advice to employees. You could be setting yourself up for conflict. However, the plan sponsor may at times allow an investment advisor to help participants with some individual investment advice. This is a complex issue, and plan sponsors who wish to supply advice to participants should proceed with prudence—and possibly seek legal advice.

DISCLOSURES

The education of participants includes the disclosure of fees and various other annual reporting requirements. Every year you should be sending them a 404(a)(5) fee-disclosure report that explains the fees charged to the plan by the mutual funds. The disclosure provides some statistics on the funds, including the rates of return, a comparison of their expense compared to the market average, and other details.

It's good information, even though few will be inclined to read it. Often they will shrug, figuring it's just some complex legal disclosure, and delete the email or throw the notice in the trash. As part of your education program, you should show the participants how to read the form and explain what is important and why. We have found it helpful to dedicate meetings to just teaching people how to read their statements and understand the plan disclosures.

The participants may also be confused by their quarterly statements. Those statements have no standard format—some are just a couple of pages, others much longer. Some are easy to understand, while others seem as if they were designed only for the chief financial officer. Some companies mail out the statement along with a newsletter, and some email it. Do what you can to prevent participants from just discarding this information. They should read it, track it, and understand it.

At a minimum, the quarterly statement must show the employee's contributions and beginning and end balances. It should identify and specifically enumerate any fees. I like to see a list that shows any advisory fees, TPA fees, and recordkeeper fees. That communicates to the participants that people are working behind the scenes and that these plans do come with an operating cost.

The DOL has been pushing for more information in the quarterly statements, although none of its guidance has become a requirement. The guidance suggests that a good addition to the statement is an asset-allocation pie chart. Another would be a graph showing the amount of contributions and their current value. That helps participants to see clearly whether the plan has been working for them. I also like to see the rate of return in the statement. Many people do not know how to calculate that accurately, particularly when considering employer contributions.

I have also been seeing statements that include a calculation that predicts how much income the balance might produce at age sixty-five. It's helpful information, similar to what you find on a Social Security statement. It can be hard to predict a future income stream based on your pool of assets today, but it can help guide participants in their financial decisions.

From Good to Great

My aim in this book has been to both caution you and encourage you. Yes, you are assuming a manageable liability risk by offering a retirement plan to your employees—but businesses live with inherent operational liability every day. If you are not careful, prudent, and proactive about your plan management, you could get fined and you could get sued. Across the land, the regulators have become more aggressive and the litigators more contentious.

The ERISA regulations exist for a reason, and the agencies that enforce them are trying to stand up for the spirit of the law, which is to protect workers from the abuses and neglect of the past. That spirit is the driving force, as well, behind the new fiduciary rules. The government wants to reassure workers that those who are helping them prepare for retirement have their best interests in mind.

As a plan sponsor, isn't that what you want for your workers as well? The regulations can be frustrating and the litigation threat can be intimidating, but remember why you set up your plan. It is likely that you wanted to attract and keep quality employees and reward them with a program that would see them through to the retirement of their dreams.

Those ideals are worthwhile. In the words of the celebrated business consultant Jim Collins, it is time now to make the leap from "good to great." You will need some help as you try to navigate these uncertain waters, but you do not want to turn back. Raise your hand, and get the assistance that you need. Your people are depending on you to do the right thing. You need to persevere as you protect yourself with knowledge and good counsel, intent on improving your retirement plan for the benefit of all.

THE RETIREMENT PLAN X-RAY IN ACTION

PLAN OVERVIEW:

ABC Management Company established a 401(k) plan in 1998 and switched it to the well-known HK Insurance Company in 2009. The plan document names ABC's president as fiduciary.

Of 168 eligible employees, eighty-eight participate. Eight former employees (retired and separated) still hold a balance. Plan assets total about $7 million. Employees receive a company match, and the plan allows loans and hardship withdrawals. Overall, the company feels the retirement plan is generous.

To simplify things and lower ABC's costs, all plan expenses except the yearly audit are paid out of plan assets. The company pays for the audit, which is required because more than a hundred employees are eligible. The CFO's small accounting firm, which he runs part time for "friends and family," does the audit at a greatly reduced cost.

A local, well-established TPA does the yearly testing and 5500 tax filing. It also provides the plan document, summary plan description, and various required disclosures, such as under ERISA 404(c).

The plan advisor, from the large XYZ Brokerage Company, comes in once a year and reviews the plan with the CFO, to whom the president delegates that duty. The president feels that his travel schedule would make meetings difficult and that the CFO knows more about finances. The broker also is available several times a year to individually advise participants.

The HR director handles most daily plan activities: payroll uploads, enrollment materials, loan and hardship withdrawal approvals, and providing census and other data to the TPA.

GOVERNANCE REVIEW:

At the daily operations level, the HR director generally does a good job of enrolling employees with a welcome package including the HK enrollment kit and the employee handbook. She follows up to ensure payroll deferrals, and the matches begin. She promptly approves or denies all loan/hardship requests. She notifies participants that they can request copies of the plan document and summary plan description. Employees promptly receive all required disclosures from HK or the TPA, either electronically or on paper.

PROBLEM AREAS:

- New enrollees are not sent a copy of the summary plan description, nor do they get any of the other required disclosures: QDIA notice, 404(c) notice, 404(a)(5) cost disclosure.

- The HR director is approving/denying loan and hardship requests. This can make the director a "functional fiduciary."

At the fiduciary level, meetings between the plan advisor and the CFO are fairly cursory. They cover general plan metrics, review performance of markets over the year, and briefly discuss plan costs and the investment menu. They emphasize covering all required asset classes (and more, often with multiple funds) to remain eligible for HK's "fiduciary-guarantee" policy.

PROBLEM AREAS:

- The president is not at the meetings and is ignoring his named fiduciary duty to monitor the plan. The CFO probably is not a fiduciary, unless his actions make him one.

- No official retirement plan committee is identified as fiduciaries. The haphazard arrangement between the president and CFO is insufficient, and it is not documented.

- The plan lacks an investment policy statement and a defined process to monitor investments.

- The CFO at least tacitly is relying on the advisor to monitor investments—but the advisor, like most brokers, is not a plan fiduciary.

- Nor is HK Insurance a plan fiduciary, despite its "fiduciary guarantee." Offered in many insurance-based plans, such a clause neither creates fiduciary status nor covers more than a single area of plan governance—and it's highly limited and after the fact.

- HK Insurance has an internal "fund-quality" scoring system, which, even if the advisor used it, would not be independent because the insurer is self-scoring. Nor is there even a rudimentary IPS in which the scoring system would be accepted as the standard.

- The discussion of plan costs is too cursory. The plan relies on revenue sharing to pay for all of the recordkeeping and part of the TPA services. They don't discuss that, feeling it doesn't matter as long as the total comes out the same. The true cost of recordkeeping and TPA costs is obscured by appearing simply as higher investment costs. Plan sponsors/fiduciaries are required to know not just total plan costs but an accurate breakdown of those costs by service provider.

- Neither the president nor CFO has put the plan out to competitive bid since signing on with HK Insurance in 2009. Many plan costs since have declined substantially. They lack even a basic point of comparison to establish if plan costs meet the DOL's "reasonability" standard for services provided.

- Meetings are not documented. No detailed notes are created or filed, and decisions are not documented. The HK-provided sponsor-review package is placed in a file folder without any meeting notes.

Auditing services problem area: Using the CFO's firm as auditor could be seen as a prohibited transaction or at least a conflict of interest, given his position at ABC and his involvement in overseeing the plan.

Participant advice problem area: The advisor's individual advice to participants could be interpreted as "undue influence," since he could be selling products for commission.

INVESTMENT QUALITY:

A detailed review of the plan's investment quality and "homeostatic" allocation uses an independent fund-scoring system of the plan's current seventy-six investment choices.

Fund Quality Level	Number of Funds	Assets in these Funds
High quality	35	$2 million
"Watchlist"	21	$1.1 million
"Remove"	20	$1.5 million
Guaranteed Acct.	20	$2.4 million

PROBLEM AREAS:

Twenty of the funds, representing over 20 percent of total assets, score below the minimum-quality threshold and should be seriously considered for removal. They should be replaced with a higher-scoring fund, or the assets should be rolled into a similar fund of higher quality already on the menu.

Other issues:

- Far too many fund options are offered. This confuses participants and makes monitoring a daunting task for the plan sponsor.

- Because the sponsor/fiduciaries never before used independent scoring, they are likely to find the results shocking.

- A large number of high-quality funds does not offset the sponsor's fiduciary responsibility to remove low-quality or inappropriate investments.

- Neither the sponsor nor advisor ever investigated whether lower-cost share classes were available on HK's platform.

- The plan lacks an IPS to define investment quality standards congruent with a scoring system that will be adopted for monitoring the menu.

- The natural or "homeostatic" allocation of funds between different investment choices indicates a heavy reliance on the insurance company's "guaranteed" account. Participants may be overwhelmed by the number of choices or lack education and knowledge to make good decisions.

RECOMMENDATIONS:

Many high-quality 401(k) platforms are available. Often, a plan's major shortcomings are not at the platform level, so switching providers would not fix the issues—much in the way a high-performance car does not make you a better driver. HK's platform may be a good choice for the company—that's still to be determined.

At this point, improving how the plan is governed and monitored likely will have the most influence on quality and compliance.

- A formal fiduciary structure should identify all plan fiduciaries and their duties. A retirement plan committee consisting of the president and CFO could be chartered to regularly review the plan with the advisor. As fiduciary, the president cannot ignore his duties but can share them with others such as the CFO. Committee members can be added as appropriate, carefully documenting their tenure as fiduciaries.

- Meeting minutes and notes should be filed along with all supporting materials (electronic copies are perfectly acceptable). The notes should document the rationale for all decisions.

- All appropriate disclosures, including the summary plan description and 404(a)(5) participant cost disclosure, must be included in an up-to-date enrollment kit. This initial interaction must be done right. Documents provided by others must incorporate *all* plan costs—such as the TPA costs—not just fund and recordkeeping charges. An incomplete disclosure is deficient.

- The employee handbook must be kept consistent with the plan document and summary. It's probably better to simply state "see summary plan description" in the handbook.

- An independent plan-auditing firm should do the yearly audit, even if that is more expensive than using the CFO's firm. The potential for conflict is too high.

- Plan costs and services need to be reviewed and understood in detail, including a breakdown of revenue sharing. The sponsor then can accurately determine whether each provider's costs are appropriate for the level of services. This sponsor has not sought competitive proposals since 2009. It typically should be done every three to four years.

- The sponsor could request, in writing, cost reductions from each provider, including less-expensive share classes from the recordkeeper. Service providers have little incentive to automatically reduce prices, even if a plan's growth justifies it. Often, simply asking can result in better pricing and additional services.

- The IPS should codify an investment-monitoring system to be used regularly, with prompt action. Faithful monitoring is critical in plan governance.

- It would be far better to offer, say, fifteen high-quality funds, monitored faithfully, than the current menu of seventy-six funds of spotty quality with little or no monitoring. The participant would get greater quality and simplicity, and the sponsor would find compliance easier.

- The sponsor should consider an alternate arrangement for individual participant advice. A broker's "undue influence" could reflect on the sponsor. The participant should not perceive that the sponsor endorses the individual advice, particularly when the advisor could get fees and commissions from product sales. A better arrangement could be one in which the advisor receives level compensation. It's fine for the advisor to provide *generalized* advice and education.

Smaller companies often lack time and resources and prefer expedience in the oversight and governance of a retirement plan. Problems usually result from neglect, not abuse. They are doing their best given their time and resources. For this sponsor, a comprehensive advisory relationship could help tremendously. It is highly recommended that the sponsor work with a fiduciary-level 3(38) investment manager to provide both of the following:

1. Independent and complete investment monitoring and management services, acting as an ERISA 3(38) investment manager. That would include creating an IPS

to regularly and consistently follow. Such an advisor can transfer liability exposure away from the plan sponsor while maintaining a quality fund menu. The additional cost of a 3(38) advisor is typically nominal over the cost of a nonfiduciary-level advisor, and it is not difficult to change advisors.

2. A comprehensive fiduciary process within the organization. This sponsor clearly is inclined toward a "please do it for me" approach. An advisor familiar with such governance processes comes equipped with necessary documents, templates, and procedures—simplifying tasks to the point where the sponsor may need only review, understand, and approve. The advisor can build a "fiduciary file" of all relevant documentation and keep the sponsor and fiduciaries abreast of regulatory changes. It can be a much less cumbersome process—clear, consistent, and repeatable—that assures high plan quality into the future.

12b-1 fee. An annual marketing or distribution fee on a mutual fund. The 12b-1 fee is considered an operational expense and, as such, is included in a fund's expense ratio.

active fund. A mutual fund that uses an active manager to select securities based on a particular style with the goal of returning more than an index or managing risk that would be less than an index.

auditor. A person/firm appointed and authorized to examine accounts and accounting records of a 401(k) or 403(b) plan when the plan exceeds one hundred eligible participants.

balanced fund. A mutual fund that includes several asset classes, usually stocks and bonds in a fixed (non-glide path, see "TDF") allocation.

basis points. A unit of measure used in finance to describe the percentage change in the value or rate of a financial instrument. One basis point is equivalent to 0.01 percent (1/100th of a percent) or 0.0001 in decimal form.

broker (non-fiduciary FINRA registered). An individual or firm that charges a fee or commission for executing buy and sell orders submitted by an investor. Typically, in management of retirement plans, brokers do not act as a fiduciary.

custodian. A financial institution that holds customers' securities for safekeeping to minimize the risk of their theft or loss. A custodian holds securities and other assets in electronic or physical form. Since they are responsible for the safety of assets and securities that may be worth hundreds of millions or even billions of dollars, custodians generally tend to be large and reputable firms.

Department of Labor (DOL). The Department of Labor is a US government cabinet body responsible for the enforcement of ERISA.

designated investment alternative (DIA). Any investment menu option available in a plan is usually considered a DIA.

Employee Retirement Income Security Act (ERISA). Protects the retirement assets of Americans by implementing rules that qualified plans must follow to ensure that plan fiduciaries comply with fiduciary responsibilities and do not misuse plan assets.

> **ERISA Section 3(21).** Any individual is a fiduciary under **Section 3(21)** if he or she exercises any authority or control over the management of the plan or the management or disposition of its assets; if he or she renders investment advice for a fee (or has any authority or responsibility to do so); or if he or she has any discretionary responsibility in the administration of the retirement plan.

> **ERISA Section 3(38).** Defines "investment manager" as a fiduciary due to their responsibility to manage the plan's assets. ERISA provides that a plan sponsor can delegate the responsibility (and thus, likely the liability) of selecting, monitor-

ing, and replacing investments to a 3(38) investment manager/ fiduciary. A 3(38) fiduciary may only be a bank, an insurance company, or a registered investment adviser (RIA) subject to the Investment Advisers Act of 1940.

ERISA Section 404(c). Section in ERISA that, among other things, provides relief from a plan sponsor having custody and responsibility for investing a participant's assets by providing a broad range of investment types and choices.

expense ratio. A measure of what it costs an investment company to operate a mutual fund. An expense ratio is determined through an annual calculation, where a fund's operating expenses are divided by the average dollar value of its assets under management. Operating expenses are taken out of a fund's assets and lower the return to a fund's investors.

fiduciary. A person who holds a legal or ethical relationship of trust with one or more other parties (person or group of persons). Typically, a fiduciary prudently takes care of money or other assets for another person.

FINRA. Financial Industry Regulatory Authority.

index fund. A mutual fund that seeks to mimic the returns of a particular stock or bond index by owning the same securities with the same weighting of each security as is represented by an index.

market up/down capture. The rate of over or underperformance of a fund relative to an index measured as a percentage of up or down performance.

net asset value (NAV). A mutual fund's price per share or exchange-traded fund's (ETF) per-share value after daily expense fees are removed. In both cases, the per-share dollar amount of the fund is calculated by dividing the total value of all the securities in its portfolio, minus any fees, by the number of fund shares outstanding.

plan sponsor. A designated party, usually a company or employer, that sets up a retirement plan such as a 401(k) or 403(b) for the benefit of the organization's employees. The responsibilities of the plan sponsor include determining membership parameters, investment choices, and, in some cases, providing contribution payments.

qualified default investment alternative (QDIA). An investment alternative (DIA) that is designated by a plan sponsor or fiduciary for investment by a participant who has not made any choice from the investment menu. A QDIA can be a target-date fund, managed account, or balanced fund.

recordkeeper. A vendor to the plan that provides services that identify each participant's proportional share of assets of the plan.

Registered Investment Advisor. Defined by the Investment Advisers Act of 1940 as a "person or firm that, for compensation, is engaged in the act of providing advice, making recommendations, issuing reports or furnishing analyses on securities, either directly or through publications." An investment advisor has a fiduciary duty to his or her clients, which means that he or she has a fundamental obligation to provide suitable investment advice and always act in the clients' best interests.

revenue sharing. The practice of sharing fees, usually derived out of mutual fund fees, to pay for other services by other service providers to a plan.

share class. A designation that identifies a fees structure for a mutual fund or similar investment. Each mutual fund will invest in the same securities but have differing fees associated with each share class. Typically, share classes with lower fees require higher initial investment.

target-date fund (TDF). A mutual fund that is generally identified by the year a participant is expected to retire. TDFs blend asset classes based on the general concept (glide path) that a more secure allocation is preferable as a participant moves closer to retirement.

third-party administrator (TPA). An organization that administrates a 401(k) or 403(b) by completing annual compliance functions including testing and tax return preparation as well as plan document creation and amendments.

ABOUT THE AUTHOR

G. David Biddle, AIF® founded Biddle Capital Management (BCM) in 1996 after several very successful years at a traditional sales-based financial firm. BCM's initial emphasis was on fee-based investment and financial advice, focused on the client. Dave was an advocate for the fiduciary concept that was budding in the late 1990s. The early client focus was on retirees and pre-retirees to provide them with independent advice for a secure future.

As the fiduciary concept grew and the investment management process at BCM matured, there was an obvious link with ERISA 401(k) retirement plan management. Dave was one of a limited number of advisors who were serving retirement plans as a fiduciary. Eventually, BCM Retirement Solutions was established as a division of BCM to support and help manage 401(k) plans. A specific division was needed to develop and support all the complex fiduciary requirements of retirement plans. After the 2006 ERISA law amendments that brought 403(b) plans into similar compliance with 401(k) plans, Dave began to educate and assist nonprofit 403(b) plan sponsors in upgrading their plans as well.

The BCM fiduciary investment management process that started in 1996 has been upgraded and improved upon as tools and fiduciary concepts have developed. The BCM fiduciary process is used for both individual clients and retirement plan clients today, resulting in advice and management that is independent and client focused.

Dave has been a featured speaker and author who is passionate about educating retirement plan sponsors on both their compliance requirements and best practices to better their 401(k) plan.

Recent speaking events:

- Brandywine 403(b) workshop, founder and presenter

- Delaware Association of Independent Schools

- Pennsylvania Association of Independent School Business Officers Association

- Brandywine 401(k) workshop, presenter

- various presentations for CPA and legal firms in the mid-Atlantic region

Recent certifications and awards:

- Accredited Investment Fiduciary (AIF®)

- multiyear awards for "Five-Star Wealth Manager"